RELIGION AND WORLD PEACE

RELIGION AND WORLD PEACE

Dr. Ravindra Kumar

GYAN PUBLISHING HOUSE
NEW DELHI-110002

Religion and World Peace

ISBN: 81-212-0903-X

Rs. 360

Published in 2006 in India by
Gyan Publishing House
5, Ansari Road, Daryaganj, New Delhi-110002
Phones : 23261060, 23282060, Fax : 91-011-23282060
E-mail : books@gyanbooks.com
Website : http://www.gyanbooks.com

Laser Typesetting at: Master Computers, Delhi
Printed at: Salasar Imaging System, Delhi

FOREWORD

Dr. Ravindra Kumar's book on religion and peace is a remarkable and valuable work on religion, spiritualism and philosophy. The author has endeavoured to explain the ideal, aims and objectives of religion and high human values, which are necessary for world peace.

All religious books and the preachings of various saints and sages of India and other countries, like Lord Rama, Lord Krishna, Lord Buddha, Jesus Christ, Prophet Mohammed, Lord Mahavira, Guru Nanak Dev etc., have given similar message of universal love, brotherhood and peace for the upliftment of mankind.

Undoubtedly, religion has an important place in the human life and it joins the heart to hearts. Religion inspires people to lead an ideal and peaceful life. All the Hindus, Muslims, Christians and Sikhs offer prayers to one and the same God for bestowing love, peace unity and prosperity. Thus, all religious communities are equal and sacred and everybody should pay respect to all other religious communities and should refrain from criticism.

In the end, I would like to say that it is need of the hour that people should follow the path of religion and lead an ideal and peaceful life based on universal love, brotherhood and unity.

I extend my good wishes for the success of this remarkable work of Dr. Ravindra Kumar.

—B. Satyanarayan Reddy

A WORD TO THE READERS

I have been writing, editing or presenting research work on vivid aspects of life of those freedom fighters for more than a decade who sacrificed their all for freedom of the country and for the oppressed and suppressed people. My sole ambition behind this work has been to bring before the people their spirit of dedication, selfless sacrifices and deep love for the masses. My attempt is directed towards bringing such persons to forefront and to present their dedicated works: the works of these great persons. In addition, my aim is to tell myself and like-minded persons the responsibility so that we are able to investigate and know their works and accord a presentation in beneficial way before ensuing generations. I cherish compliments of readers and beseech that I shall try to present nice works in future.

Recently, I have passed through many bitter experiences of life. I derived might out of them and I could get a chance to know realities of life. During my life-tenure I have also attempted to grasp and understand different religious communities that are present on this earth. While doing so, I tried to know main points of them from time to time-especially, in context of world peace.

I feel that I could not fully achieve my ambition. It is my first attempt in the field of religion. I beseech all learned persons to please accept it along with a spirit to ignore the mistakes committed considering that it is my first attempt in this direction.

—Ravindra Kumar

INTRODUCTION

Religion is at the very basis of human life. Religion influences every human action and behaviour and so it affects the very activity of human life. Whatever explanations and meanings of the fundamental basis of life be given, and since whenever we may accept its very existence, we cannot but accept this fact that *'religion'* has been the source of establishing peace in the world that means peace for all human beings.

There is no denying the fact that there is difference of opinion about the ingredients of religion. This is also true that different opinions have been expressed about the presence of the mode of worship in different religious communities and so far as their role in the establishment of universal peace is concerned, there is no scope for dissension or conflict. Thus it is amply clear that religion determines the sole human aim of the establishment of universal peace. That is why Lord Buddha remarked that it is better to listen to one religious *pada* which is fountain-head of peace and tranquillity than lending one's ear to meaningless hundred tales comprising of a thousand *padas*.

Each word, each message and each invocation emanating from a religious community is a step towards the establishment of stable peace and that is what every propounder of a religious community has been placing before the world. Religion cannot be blamed if the world today is strife-torn, if there are differences of opinion; and if ideals of humanity are on the decline. Those who have gone astray and who have neglected the strong calls of religion for the establishment of world peace are to be blamed and those who while interpreting the meaning of religion forget to explain that the path of world peace emanates from its very root are to be blamed.

Only this peace can become the source of succour and salvation. The religion which talk of salvation of soul, first of all call upon the people to help establish peace in every sphere of human life and talk of anything else only thereafter. Here I am not dwelling upon the meaning of religion or talking of salvation. What I want to emphasise is that if we go to the depth of Christ's '*SERMON ON THE MOUNT*', we shall certainly find that it also lays emphasis on the establishment of universal peace. In this context, its immortal message is: "*Love your enemies and pray for them that persecute you, for that you may be the sons of your father who is in Heaven.*"

Undoubtedly, it is the message of peace. Even Confucius-the great philosopher had stated thousands of years ago that establishment of peace is the biggest duty of man and for the achievement of this aim he should do good and should also expect the same from others. He emphasised on the need of permanent peace for everybody and opposed the very desire of peace for self at the cost of peace for everybody and stated:

"*Don't behave with others in the manner in which you don't want others to behave with you. If you don't want your peace to be spoiled then don't spoil others' peace.*"

We should understand the very essence of religion through this message of peace.

The message of universal brotherhood contained in Hinduism definitely aims at directing the globe on the path of stable peace. The very idea of equality among humans hints at the establishment of world peace. Mahatma Gandhi, in this context, was absolutely right. By expecting of Hinduism, he sated:

"In the purest terms Hinduism considers a Brahmin, an ant, an elephant and a dog at the same level. Hinduism advocates brotherhood not only among the human beings but among all the living beings as well. This really is a fantastic idea but we have to put it into real practice. We shall be able to establish a proper equality among the human beings and the universe when we are able to achieve equality among men in the real sense of the word. The ushering in of such an order would establish a regime of peace in the world and that of goodwill among men."

Zoroaster-the propounder of Zoroastrianism, was aghast to see strife and conflict in the world and he aimed at choosing a path of his own for the establishment of world peace. Like Buddha and Mahavira, Zoroaster too contemplated in order to delve deep into the mysteries of human life which right from birth to death is enveloped with sorrows. The disparities in the world among the rich and the poor, first of all, made him to think on this issue. He wanted to know why the world was full of sorrow and despairs and why there was conflict and strife in this world. He found the way to get peace and, in his first sermon, said:

"The evil is the root cause of all the conflicts. There is a yawning gap between what men say and what they really do and this is the root cause of our sorrows and miseries."

How can we change this situation? In the words of Zoroaster himself :

> *"These miseries can be removed if man is able to differentiate between good deeds and evil deeds, fears God and feels contented with what he has. Thus [by doing so]*

he will be at peace and shall certainly be able to work for the world peace."

Not only this, Zoroaster went to the extent of saying that "*the very existence of man is linked with the world peace.*"

All the great prophets, godly men and propounders of different religious communities have not only given the message of establishment of peace in the world but terming it to be the true human duty and also they worked for it. Their only aim was the establishment of peace in the world. If we find anything relating to violence during the times of Lord Rama, Lord Krishna or Prophet Mohammed, its only aim was to establish peace and use of force must have been the only alternative under the given conditions. Those who wish to establish peace cannot be blamed if they take some violent measures against those who are bent upon bringing destruction. The only thing is that they should act with a clear heart. In this context Lord Krishna himself has said in *shloka* 17 of chapter 18 of the *Gita* :

> "*As it is no violence if fire, air and water do not act in violence against somebody just in the same manner if a person who does not take pride in his possession and who acts selflessly for the welfare of mankind, it is no violence even if his actions amount to violence in the eyes of the people in general. Because there can be no violence without the ills of attachment, selflessness and pride and any action done without pride is no action and therefore the said person is sinless.*"

Jainism which lays strong emphasis over non-violence always wishes for peace at every level and establishes such principles so as to lead the world on the path of peace. Lord Mahavira has recommended five resolves in order to establish peace:

"To refrain from taking life; from speaking untrue words; for taking what is not willingly given; from all unlawful love; from ownership of goods and limits of strict need."

Similarly, Moses-the propounder of Judaism emphasising over the establishment of world peace has stated:

"Thou shall not kill,

Not bear false witness,

Not steal,

Not commit adultery,

*Not covet anything that is thy neighbour'*s."

Thus we arrive at the conclusion that each religious community has the fundamental lesson of establishment of peace to teach. There may be difference of opinion regarding the method of achieving this aim but there is no difference at all so far as their aim of establishment of world peace is concerned.

The problem of strife and conflict in this world is a matter of great concern and each religious community offers solution for it. Then why should we not follow the principles of our own religious faith and by adhering to those tenets should make life peaceful and comfortable. I am not saying something new. All the followers of different faiths too make a fervent appeal in this regard.

I strongly believe that we should recognise the real shape of religion. With my personal study of different faiths coupled with the results that I have arrived at from the correspondence I have had with great men of the world on the subject of establishment of world peace, I strongly feel that only religion can play a decisive and useful role in the establishment of world peace.

This work on religion and peace is my first attempt in this direction in order to bring to common reader the immortal message of various religious communities. I am a very humble man and do not claim scholarship or specialisation in the field of religion or religious communities; it is just an attempt. In the event of availability of sufficient resources and proper opportunity in future, I shall continue to work in this direction.

In this study, I have tried to explain the basic principles of Buddhism, Christianity, Hinduism, Islam, Jainism, Sikhism and Zoroastrianism for the establishment of world peace. I have also tried to present their practical aspects too. However, there are many other religious communities too in the world which like these also aim at the establishment of world peace.

The sources of inspiration for me for this study have been Lord Rama, Lord Krishna, Lord Zoroaster, Lord Mahavira, Lord Buddha, Lord Moses, Lord Jesus Christ, Prophet Mohammed, Guru Nanak Dev, Swami Ramakrishna 'Paramahansa', Swami Vivekananda, Leo Tolstoy, Mahatma Gandhi and many other great men. I am of the opinion that all of them had the sole aim of relieving mankind of all the miseries and sorrows and of leading them on to the path of permanent and stable peace and this is the only path of common good.

I am grateful to a number of great scholars and saints for their useful co-operation in the preparation of this work. I thank from the core of my heart His Holiness the 14th Dalai Lama, Tenzin Gyatso, His Holiness, the Pope John Paul II, His Holiness, Maulana Syed Abul Hasan Ali Nadvi, His Holiness, Shri Shrimad Bhakti Vedanta Swami

Prabhupad, His Holiness, Jainacharya Muni Vidyanand, Shri S. G. Mohiuddin, Dr. Hari Singh, Miss Adyth Banks, Jain Sadhvi Dr. Manjushri, Jain Sadhvi Akshayshri 'Akha', Shri Babubhai Jashbhai Patel, Shri David Prabhudas, Mufti Shamshuddin Ahmed, Shri V. B. Pant, Shri K. P. Shiv Kumar, D. Multani, Maj. Pull, V. Phull, B. Kaur, Shri V. B. Pant, Shri Sharad Agrawal and others in the preparation of this work and for their cooperation.

Before putting a full stop, I want to say some thing about my views pertaining to religion. As I have already stated, in Hindi edition too, Zoroastrianism, Sikhism, Shintoism, Judaism, Jainism, Islam, Hinduism, Confucianism, Christianity or Buddhism- all are religious communities. They may have different methods of worship but have many nice attributes, as such; they all are a part of religion. I shall be a very happy man if this attempt succeeds in revealing the true message of the religious communities for their followers. I am respectful to them all.

—Ravindra Kumar

CONTENTS

ABBREVIATIONS

A. I. D. S.	:	Acquired Immune Deficiency Syndrome
A. M. U.	:	Aligarh Mulsim University
B. C.	:	Before Christ
A. D.	:	After The Death of Christ
S. M.	:	Sahitya Mandal

CHAPTER-1
BUDDHISM

Understanding the Reality of the World Having Four Great Truths in the Centre

Gautama–the Buddha, in the 100th *pada* of *Dhammapada* remarks:

"One meaningful pada which is the source of peace and tranquillity is far better than meaningless padas and thousand sentences."[1]

Further he states that lending one's ear to one religious *pada,* which is the fountainhead of tranquillity, is better than listening to the hundred tales composed of meaningless *padas.*

This amply proves that the Buddha attached utmost importance to human power and did not like the sentence which drew man away from internal peace. Moreover, he would not think of such a religion which failed to establish peace. It is quite clear from the second couplet:

"A pada which provides inner peace is worth adopting."

It is broadly clear that what does not provide peace is not religion. That is why the Buddha considered religion the basis that accords peace to man and relieves him of sorrows which surround him.

It is universally known that Buddhism, in order to establish world peace, first of all moves towards the human sorrows and is of the opinion that *'sorrow exists', 'there is cause of sorrow', 'sorrow could be rooted out'* and *'there could be means for the cessation of sorrow'.* These are considered the four great [noble] truths of the Buddhism. It would not be out of place to define these truths in the words of His Holiness, the Dalai Lama who has rightly pointed out that the root of Buddhism is the four noble truths–sufferings, sources, cessations and paths. The four truths are two groups of effect and cause: suffering and their sources and cessations of sufferings and the path for actualizing those cessations. Suffering is like an illness; the external and internal conditions that bring about illness are the source of suffering. The state of cure from the illness is the cession of suffering and of its cause. The medicine that cures the disease is true path.

The reason for this order with the effect, suffering and cession before the causes, sources of suffering and path, is like this: Initially you must identify the illness, true suffering the first noble truth. Then, it is not sufficient just to recognize the illness; in order to know which medicine to take it is necessary to know the cause of illness. Therefore, the second of the four truths is the cause of sources of suffering.

It is not sufficient just to identify the cause of illness; you need to determine whether it is possible to cure the disease. Knowledge that it can be cured is similar to the third level, that of true cessation of suffering and its causes.

Now, the unwanted suffering has been recognized; its causes have been identified; then, at the point at which it is understood that the illness can be cured, you take the medicines that are the means for removing the illness. Similarly, it is necessary to rely on the paths which bring about the state of freedom from suffering.

It is considered most important initially to identify suffering. Suffering in general, is of three types:

- The suffering of pain;
- The suffering of change; and
- Pervasive compositional suffering.

The suffering of pain is what we usually consider to be physical or mental suffering, for instance a headache. The wish to be free from this type of suffering occurs not just in humans but also in animals. There are ways of avoiding some forms of this suffering, such as taking medicines, putting on warm clothes, and moving away from the source.

The second level, the suffering of change, is what we superficially consider to be in pleasure but which, if we look into it, is actually suffering. Take as an example something usually considered be to pleasurable, such as buying a new car. When you first get it, you are happy, pleased and satisfied but then as you use it, problems arise. If it were intrinsically pleasurable, no matter how much more you used this cause of satisfaction, your pleasure should increase correspondingly, but such does not happen. As you use it more and more, it begins to cause trouble. Therefore, such things are called sufferings of change; it is through change that their nature of suffering is displayed. The third level of suffering serves as the basis of the first two, and what illustrates it are our own contaminated mental and physical aggregates. It is called pervasive compositional suffering since it pervades or applies to all types of transmigrating beings and is compositional in that it is the basis of present suffering and induces future suffering. There is no way of getting away from this type of suffering except by ending the continuum of rebirth.

These are the three types of suffering to be identified in the beginning. Thus, not just feelings are identified as suffering but also the external and internal phenomena is dependent upon which such feelings come; the mind and mental factors that accompany them are designed as suffering as well.

What are the sources of these sufferings? In dependence on what does suffering arise? These are :

- *Karmic* Sources; and
- Sources which are the affective emotion.

These above are the second of the four noble truths, true sources of suffering. *Karma* or action refers to contaminated physical, verbal and mental action. From the point of view of nature of entity, actions are of three types:

- Virtuous: Virtuous actions are those that issue forth pleasurable or good effects;
- Non-virtuous: Non-virtuous actions are those that issue forth painful or bad effects; and
- Neutral.

The three main affiictive emotions are:

- Obscuration;
- Desire; and
- Hatred.

These induce many other varieties of afflictive emotions such as jealousy and enmity. In order to cease the *karmas* or actions that are a source of suffering, it is necessary to cease the afflictive emotions which act as their cause. Therefore, betwixt *karmas* and afflictive emotions the main source of suffering is the latter, afflictive emotions.

When you question whether the afflictive emotions can be removed or not? , you are concerned with the third noble truth-true cessations. If afflictive emotions resided in the very nature of the mind, it would be impossible to remove them. If hatred, for example, resides in the nature of the mind, then as long as we are conscious we should be hateful, but this is obviously not the case. The same is true for attachment, therefore, it is considered that the nature of mind; of consciousness, is not polluted by defilements. The defilements are susceptible to being removed, suitable to be separated from the basic mind.

It is obvious that the good class of attitude is contradictory with the bad class of attitudes. For example, love and anger cannot be generated exactly at the same time in the same person. While you are feeling anger with respect to an object at that very instant you cannot feel love; similarly, while you are feeling love, at that moment you cannot feel anger. This indicates that these two types of consciousness are mutually exclusive, contradictory. Thus, naturally, once you become more accustomed to one class of attitudes, the other class becomes weaker and weaker. This is the reason why through practising and increasing compassion and love- the good side of thought- the other side automatically diminishes. In this way, it is established that the sources of suffering can gradually be removed. With the utter extinction of the causes of suffering, there is true cession. This is the final liberation-real, lasting peace, salvation. It is the third of the four noble truths.

In what kind of path should you train to achieve this cession? Since faults mainly derive from the mind, the antidote must be generated mentally. Indeed, you need to know the final mode subsistence of all phenomena, but it is most important to know the final status of mind.

First you need to realize directly and in a totally non-dualistic manner the final nature of the mind exactly as it is; this is called the path of seeing. Then, the next level is to become used to the perception; this is called the path of meditation. Prior to these two levels, it is necessary to achieve a dualistic meditative stabilization which is union of calm abiding and special insight. Prior to that, generally speaking in order to have a powerful wisdom consciousness it is necessary first to develop stability of mind, called calm abiding.

These are the levels of the path, the forth noble truth, required for actualizing the third noble truth, cessations that are states of having ceased the first two noble truths-sufferings and their sources. The four truths are the basic structure of Buddhist thought and practice.

Now, after understanding the spirit of the great four truths, we should take those features of Buddhism which are of great help in the establishment of world peace and are related to its practical aspect which unites the whole mankind.

◇ UNDERSTANDING THE REALITY OF THE WORLD

What is human life? It is our first and foremost duty to understand its reality because there can be no cessation of human sorrows and the consequent establishment of peace till the whole society continues to be prey to violence and differences between the human beings are on the rise. The Buddha pointed out in this context :

"*Why smile when everything is afire? Why these rejoicings? Why don't you search the lamp of devotion when there is darkness all around* ?"[2]

In another illustration where Buddha satirises the human body :

"*Look at this body, its condition is highly precarious; it is full of sorrows, wants and desires.*"[3]

◇ CHANGING THE STATE OF MIND

Buddhism supports the change in the state of human mind for the promotion of peace in human life and chief change that should be affected is that of jealousy- stricken human mind with jealousy, enmity and desire of wrecking vengeance are the greatest obstacles in the path of the achievement of peace. In the words of Lord Buddha :

"*Such people are never at peace who always think in terms that so and so abused him, so and so beat him, defeated him or robbed him. The feelings of enmity of such people are never removed and they are never at peace. But those people who relieve themselves of these disturbing thoughts are relieved of the feeling of enmity.*"[4]

Not only this, the Buddha considered that the true human religion which established peace in the world had nothing to do with enmity, defeat and jealousy. He pointed out that enmity cannot remove enmity; enmity is suppressed with the help of goodwill and friendship, and this has been considered human duty since time immemorial.

◊ REMOVAL OF THE FEELING TO PUNISH AND SENSE OF EQUALITY

When the Buddha came to realize the reality of his life and was able to find the right path with the help of contemplation, he was enlightened by the eternal truth that *'LOVE AND PITY'* is the best source of self-promotion and the progress of this self-promotion helps in the establishment of world peace. That is why the Buddha gave a message of equality and strongly opposed the policy of punishment or killing. He said that everybody is afraid of punishment and death. Therefore, we should consider all living beings equal and should neither kill nor should have the desire to kill others.

The Buddha further states that everyone loves to live despite the fear of death. We should, therefore, stop thinking in terms of killing and should also control the desire to do so.

◊ EXPECTING FROM THE SELF

A person who wants peace at the cost of other's peace shall never attain it- is an old and universally accepted principle. Similarly, a society, a nation or a group of nations which even imagine to achieve peace at the cost of other's peace can never be at peace for long. The Buddha, therefore, had very clearly stated some two thousand and five hundred years ago that it is better first to mould ones self accordingly before advising others to mould themselves. First of all control yourself and only then tell others to do so. In fact, it is difficult to control oneself. In his own words:

"*Man is his own master. Nobody else can master him. This rare mastery is achieved only by controlling oneself and achieving consequent inner peace.*"[5]

The Buddha is very clear of the view that a person who wants to get joys by bringing sorrows to others can never be at peace and can never attain the joys himself.

Thus, the religious community propounded by the Buddha is based on the basic principle of the religion- the establishment of world peace. Buddhism gives the message of the termination of all the sorrows and wishes for the attainment of universal joys, which is the basic principle for the establishment of true and lasting peace. It will be proper to go through a couplet in order to understand how the Buddha loves '*peace*' which means:

"*There is no fire like attachment and no trap like envy and there can be no joy greater than peace.*"

The Buddha asked the human beings to be beware of all those causes which terminate peace, be they enmity, fear or hatred. In this regard, some of his immortal messages are hereunder:

"Live like friends among those who are inimical to you. Try to feel that we are leading a peaceful and comfortable life." What a beautiful message the Buddha has delivered to man to shake off his unfriendly state of mind. The Buddha also expressed his views about abandoning fear. It means :

"Try to be without fear among those who have fallen prey to fear. Try to feel that we are leading a comfortable life."

Living fearlessly in the community of fear afflicted people is another important message of Lord Buddha and it helps to establish peace. Hereunder is a message for people who seek indulgence:

"Remain austere among the indulgent. Feel that you are leading a comfortable life. Lead an austere life while among those who are attached."[6]

The Buddha has emphasised over the need of changing the state of mind of those who desire for more and they feel that they cannot lead a comfortable life without it. The desire to achieve is, in fact, a very bad notion of the people living in this world and this is the root of strife.

In order to *'have more'*, a man, a nation or a group of nations is prepared to exploit others and bids farewell to the fine ideals of humanity. The Buddha therefore asks people to control themselves, and their desire to develop self-contentment and thus advises:

"We don't possess anything. Try to feel that we are leading a pleasant life. Only then shall we be able to lead a godly life."[7]

The Buddha has, again and again, called upon the mortals to relinquish the sense of enmity and has given the message of living in a friendly manner. He has emphasised that nursing the '*sense of victory*' is a big hurdle in the path of peace for a man or a nation. Hence, this victory is not true as it is always accompanied by miseries. Therefore, it is essential to do away with this state of mind in order to establish peace for the welfare of one and all. In his own words:

"*Victory breeds enmity. A vanquished always lives in despair. In fact, only the one who is without any attachment and envy can have a sound sleep.*"

Thus Lord Buddha and Buddhism have left no stone unturned to establish permanent peace in the world. Hence the fundamental principle of this religious community just like other communities of the world is to direct the people from the path of destruction to the path of peace.

References

1. *Dhammapada*, 100: 8

2. Ibid 146: 11

3. Ibid 147: 11

4. Ibid 3: 1

5. Ibid 160: 12

6. Ibid 199: 15

7. *Sukha Vaggo*, 200: 15

CHAPTER-2
CHRISTIANITY

Removal of Evil to Ensure Love and Service for All

"My peace I give you
My peace I leave with you" **(Lord Jesus)**

Peace is the fundamental principal of Christianity also. Bible says to remain, obedient, to be ready to do whatever is good, to slander no one and to show true humanity towards all men. Christ's words are, *"Render unto Caeser what is Caeser's and render unto God what is God's."* When we consider the world that we live in and follow that news the pours in from every corner of our world both through the print and electronic media, we realise what a turbulent and violent phase our world is going through even now, and each day we seem to be getting further and further away from peace.

◊ THE BIBLE

A careful study of the Bible shows that there is a comprehensive answer to the various issues related to peace at personal, local, national and international level. The Bible claims to be God's divine revelation to man, this revelation involves a progressive unfolding. Even through the progressive unfolding one can see the Bible giving a total picture that answers many perplexing questions related to issues that concern peace in its various ramifications.

In Chapters I and II, of Genesis, the first book of the Bible, we get an account of the creation of the heavens and the earth and all that it contains. It also shows us that man was created by God as the crown of creation. Man, [includes women as well every time reference is made to man] was created in the image of God. By that we mean a finite copy of the infinite God, capable of communion with God. God also meant for mankind to rule over the rest of creation.

Practical implications of the important revelation in these two chapters are; that all men of the earth have one origin and are really one family. Classes and castes, superior and inferior races, lording over and suppression or the slave mentality, none of these were God's plan for mankind. The various unhappy distortions that we have today are all man-made. God's design was that man would rule over the rest of creations and not reduce the dignity of a fellow human. A surgeon doesn't see us as inferior or superior beings when operating on us, there is no such thing, a beggar on the street, a scholar, saint or scientist would all have the same constitution and consequently would require the same treatment as well. The world that God has created had order, beauty and perfection. God's comment on His creative work was that it was good.

Man was created without blemish, was placed in a perfect environment and was to rule over the rest of creation. In that perfect state that he was created in, and the ideal environment that he lived in, man might have risen to all his potential for goodness. Even today and all through history we have seen evidence of the goodness of man though this has often been eclipsed by antithetical tendencies.

In chapter III of Genesis there is an account of the fall of man. The account itself is rather simple, but the implications are of profound and far-reaching consequences.

Man, in relation to the rest of creation was a ruler. His authority, power and wisdom were given to him by God himself. Man's authority was a delegated authority. In relation to the rest of creation he was a ruler, but in relation to God he was the creature who had to submit to the authority of God. Submission is often understood in its negative connotation, but in submitting to God man was not losing his dignity was rather enhancing it, for it is only in the dimension of a right relationship with God that man experiences and discovers his true dignity and receives his authority to rule over the rest of creation.

When God created the first couple on earth, He gave them unlimited freedom but one small restriction. They were not to eat the fruit of a particular tree. This requirement was actually a test of man's obedience and consequently his submission to God.

Disobedience meant an act of rebellion. The creation can neither be like the creator nor greater and independent of the creator. One doesn't think of a light bulb shining independent of a power source or attempting to replace the power house. As long as it is reliant on the power source it can shine and be useful as well. So it is with man, as long as he is reliant upon God and submissive to Him, he does well. The sad state of affair that we find ourselves in all round with dangerously disturbed eco-systems, nuclear equipments to blow over our earth at least a hundred times to slavery, poverty, violence, AIDS, drug problems, terrorist activity, unrest, corruptions, hatred, strife, divisions; This shows that man desperately needs to bring order, dignity, beauty and peace into our world, that is badly shattered and so frighteningly lacking in hope.

◊ PHILOSOPHY OF CHRISTIANITY

As mentioned already, Christianity says that man's authority was a delegated authority. In relation to the rest of creation he was a ruler, but in relation to God he was the creature who had to submit to the authority of his creator, God.

Our very lives that are so mortal are in His hand, and we gain every privilege and exercise every right as a gift from God, and not because of any personal merit or capacity.

Genesis, Chapter III has a simple account which shows how man fell into sin. Temptation came in the form of a serpent and spoke to the woman that in eating the fruit men and women would be like God. Man was also deluded and tempted to rebel against God. The cost was awful. Creation itself fell. Thorns and thistles were to come where fruit and grain were to abound. Man was to sweat for his food. Man lost his special relationship with God, the image of God that he was created in was marred and tainted with sin, guilt and a tendency towards evil. This tendency towards evil was passed on from parent to children until the entire human beings were born with an evil nature. Because of the fall man lost his standing with God and his peace with God, as well as peace with himself and his fellowmen. With a natural bent to evil and in an environment over which, evil presides; it was only natural for a chaotic, turbulent, catastrophic environment to set in.

If Genesis chapter III describes the fall of man, chapter IV is a vivid portrayal of what such a fall can lead to. The first born of the first couple on earth slew his own younger brother in a fit of rage and jealousy. In just IV chapters of the Bible we find sufficient information to show that man was created innocent and blameless, and placed in an ideal environment. Here he could have risen to his full potential, growing in all goodness and with an absence of evil. Man did have a good start. But soon he fell, was driven away from both the ideal environment and from the protective umbrella of God and came directly under the influence of Satan whom the Bible says is the personification of evil.

Chapter IV is commentary in capsule of the kind of evil the human race is subjected to. All of our manifold problems, and our lack of peace, which is just one of the more important systems of it, are a result of sin; a result of man falling in grace and losing face before God. The problem of sin; man's inclination to evil as a result of the fall, an environment of evil that man has created through the ages and the influence of Satan and his forces upon the world and upon our lives are a key to understanding all the ills and evils of our world. But God was not to be just a silent spectator of the problems that beset the human race. Right in the context of the fall, He had made the promise of remedial measures.

◊ CONCEPT OF PEACE

Now a brief discussion on the subject of peace in the Bible and the Christianity before tracing the divine remedy for man's loss of peace and desperate need of it :

PEACE [Source: Banker's Dictionary of the Theology, Pickering and Inglis]. The primary and basic idea of the Biblical world "*peace*" is Shalom in the Old Testament, and Eirane[1] in the New Testament, is completeness, soundness and wholeness. It is a favourite Biblical greeting. It is found at the beginning or end of most of the New Testament letters. It is a common word among the Semities. Even dismissal is expressed by the word. It means cessation from war; friendship between companions as well as friendship with God through a covenant. Contentment or anything working towards safety, welfare, and happiness is included in the concept.

As said, peace has reference to health, prosperity, well-being security as well as respite from war. The Prophet Isaiah pointed out repeatedly that there will be no peace to the wicked even though many of the wicked continually seek to encourage themselves with a false peace. Peace is a condition of freedom from strife whether internal or external. Security from outward enemies as well as calm of heart for those having trust in God is included. Peace is so pleasing to the Lord that they, godly are enjoyed to seek it diligently. It must be the characteristic of the New Testament's believer also, i.e., a disciple of the Lord Jesus Christ.

Peace is a comprehensive and valued gift from God, and the promised and climaxing bliss in Messianic times. In the New Testament the word has reference to the peace which is the gift of Christ. It is used many times to express the truths of the mission, character and gospel of Christ. The purpose of Christ's coming into the world was to bring spiritual peace with God. There is sense in which He came not to bring peace, but a sword. This has reference to the struggle with every form of sin. Christ's life depicted in the gospels is one of majestic calm and serenity. The essence of the gospel may be expressed in the term peace, including the peace of reconciliation with God and the peace of fellowship with God.

The innumerable blessings of the Christianity revolve around the concept of peace. The gospel is the gospel of peace. Christ is our peace, God the father is the God of peace. The inalienable privilege of every Christian is the peace of God, because of the legacy of peace left by Christ in his death. These blessings are not benefits laid up in eternal glory only, but are a present possession. Thus, peace is "*a conception distinctly peculiar to Christianity, the tranquil state of a soul assured of its salvation through Christ, and so fearing nothing from God and content with its earthly lot, of whatever sort that is.*" At the outset, we have dealt with the subject of the fall of man and the consequences of it. Sin was traced as the cause behind all our problems and the lack of peace. Now for a discussion of the divine remedy, the justice of God demanded that men be adequately punished for their sins, but the love of God made the provision for the forgiveness of the sins of mankind.

God's solution was in the Lord Jesus Christ who is God personified He had to be conceived of the Holy Spirit and born of a virgin so that he would not be tainted with sin just like the rest of humanity is. A passing reference needs to be made to Trinity. It is normal to see references in the Bible to God the father, God the son and God the Holy Spirit. The question that naturally comes to one's mind are questions like, "*Do the Christians have more than one God*?" A definition of trinity is not easy to construct. One of the best is Warfield's, "*there is only one and true God, but in the unity of the Godhead there are three co-eternal and two-equal persons, the same in substance but distinct in subsistence.*"[2]

Lord Jesus Christ was God become man, yet truly God and truly man. He came to lay down his life as a ransom for our sins. He shed his blood and died in our place taking upon himself the punishment we deserve. Being fully man, the sacrifice of his life was adequate to pay for our sins in mind and quality, thus satisfying the divine justice of God. But being God His life is of infinite value and the sacrifice of Christ has the capacity to pay for the sins of the whole world. Being God, the Lord Jesus Christ also rose from the dead and is alive today. It is a firm belief in Christianity. That's the Great News, also called the Good News.

According to Christianity, forgiveness does not take place spontaneously or automatically. Each individual has to make a deliberate choice to accept or reject the provision. There is no precondition apart from repentance, a desire to live a life pleasing to God and a simple complete child like faith in the saving power of Christ's sacrifice for the forgiveness of one's sins; nothing more, nothing less. There's nothing else we need to do, and there's no way in which we can bribe God or buy Him. It is clear here.

The Gospel, or the Good News, is the proclamation that in Jesus Christ there is available both the forgiveness of sins and the privilege of beginning a new life. When one believes in the sacrifice of Christ on his or her behalf and accepts it, God forgives and does a work of transformation.

In Jesus Christ the image of God in man that was marred is partly remedied, and man has a new beginning. In fact, the Bible calls it a new birth. One does not get back into the womb of one's mother for that. It is a work of the Spirit and in the spiritual realm. It cannot be measured or monitored by technical equipment in a sophisticated hospital. But its result can be seen and felt by others and as well as by the one in whose life this takes place. Speaking of this the Bible says:

"Which is born of the flesh is flesh and that which is born of the spirit is spirit. The wind blows where it wishes and you hear the sound of it, but do not know where it comes from and where it is going; so is everyone who is born of the spirit."

The Bible also describes the experience in the following manner:

"*Therefore, if any man is in Christ*[3], *he is a new creature; the old things passed away; behold new things have come.*"

Christianity believes that the individual can either grow in grace and experience peace with God, peace within himself or be instrument of peace as an example, or, he can stagnate, backslide, or lose out, whatever ground that has gained can be lost. A onetime commitment for profession of faith in Christ does not become an automatic all time guarantee that all is fine ever after. It is a relationship with God that has potential for transformation all along the way.

◊ THE CHURCH

The Church, from a proper Biblical understanding of it, is not made up of a kind of images that we normally assume as being representative of it. It is not impressive building, indicate rituals, ecclesiastical structure, missions with big budgets, or the percentage-wise proportion of a particular religious group in different parts of the world but the church is a fellowship of believers. Unique, caring, growing community of believers in Jesus Christ who seek to know more of God, to worship him, to build each other in the things of God, minister to each others need and reach out to the world both with the message of the Gospel and to be as light as salt-showing the way to God and leading towards the pathway of love, justice and ultimately peace through proclamation and example, and being the salt again through effort and example.

It is true that the Church has often failed, and Christianity has often been a bad example, in ages past and even now when one considers the topic of world peace. But bearing the name Christian doesn't automatically make one Christ like or guarantee that one's life is lived under the Lordship of Christ. Nor does one automatically become a Christian by being born into a Christian home or attending Church. There are multitudes of nominal Christians whose lives may not reflect Christ. Christ is not to be blamed for that.

Yet it is true that Lord Jesus Christ was the direct motivating and sustaining factor in ever so many humanitarian's developmental and educational projects that the world and in so many ways even India too has been direct beneficiary of. As we know, quality that has become the hallmark of Christian Schools, colleges, hospitals, old age home, orphanage, development projects, technical institutes etc. is always a direct outcome of a commitment to Christ and nothing else. Where such institutions have failed or are failing, the reason invariable is that the degree of commitment to Christ is, on the decline. That way the good example and expressions of Christianity are foretaste of what can come to the world if the Good News of the Gospel is responded to.

Apart from poverty, violence and injustice are also major problems in our world. Naturally peace is absent where these are dominant. A true Christian is one who strives to follow a high standard of personal ethics, he is also one who firmly believes that love is stronger than hatred and that evil can only be overcome with good. He does all he can to help a needy and a suffering human being in humanitarian terms. It would be no exaggeration to claim that Christians have done good works in a proportion that is far in excess of their percentage in many parts of a needy and suffering world.

In fact, Christianity cannot transform or rule the world with automatic international peace, but can certainly provide examples of the ideal in small percentage wherever the true Church expresses itself. And of course no Church is perfect. The true Church is not a community of saints but a community of forgiven sinners who strive to live God-pleasing lives.

According to Christianity Order, justice and peace, in the ultimate sense cannot be achieved in the present world context. That would happen sometime in the future that God alone knows when there would be a divine intervention in human affairs. At this time the forces of evil [Satan and Fallen angles] would be bound and punished. There would be a New Heaven and New Earth. Beautiful though our world is in its natural state and in many places where man has beautified it, yet the scriptures state that the very creation groans to be redeemed. The earth was cursed with thorns and thistles when man fell. It would also be a time of reckoning when God would judge all men of all times and designate to them their reward or punishment. This involves a vast area of study known as Biblical Eschatology or the Doctrine of the last things. This is where the message of the Gospel assumes great significance.

Those who respond are blessed, those who disobey would pay the price. Those who have obeyed have a mandate to proclaim this wonderful message of the Good News of the Gospel. They are so convinced of the truth of what they believe that they proclaim often at great personal cost and even if it would cost their lives in the process. The Bible also says that it is appointed for man to die once and then the judgement. Life on earth is probation. Our decision about Christ and our response to Him now determines both the quality of our present life and our future destiny.

Now what can we do? It is true that our world is vast and the problems it faces are Himalayan and often difficult to solve. But the Bible shows that by allowing Christ to come into our lives we allow Him to change us before we can begin a process of change that would improve conditions in our world and contribute a little towards its change for a better.

◊ SIN

As mentioned, sin is at the root of the entire problem. Sin is dealt with by the grace of Lord Jesus. Once that is done, men is forgiven, changed for good, experiences peace with God and within himself, and begins to express love, hope, goodness and ultimately peace in world that doesn't have it .The Christian message is not a message that aims to add on the world's problems and complications. It is often viewed and treated as an enemy or as a threat. The truth is that the Christian proclamation has the potential to bring in good[4] and remove evil wherever it makes its impact. It may not be an exaggeration to claim that over half of the humanitarian efforts in the world after the times of Lord Christ have a Christian background to them.

A striking modern example is Mother Teresa in India who repeatedly affirms that it is the love of Jesus that makes her do what she has been doing. Through centuries, many Christians for the same reason have done similar tasks. The reward lies not in human recognition but in the joy that comes through service to the Lord and His name. Lord Jesus Christ has said that even a cup of cold water given in His name will have His reward, so His true followers know that He, in whose name they carry out acts of love and compassion [solid basis of peace] notices their deeds.

Christianity has a spontaneous attitude of service in love and compassion for the lesser privileged and for those in need. It is a way to peace. The best schools, colleges, hospitals in India had their humble beginnings with motives of service.

The essence of Christianity was conveyed in the '*Sermon*' by Lord Jesus known as the '*Sermon on the Mount*'. To sum up the formula for peace for true Christians and all humanity lies in the words of Lord Christ:

"Blessed are the peace makers"

"For they shall be called the children of God"

References

1. Old Testament in Hebrew language.

Note : Covenant is an important concept in the Bible and it does have in the ancient nearer Easter cultures as well. The concept is found in both the Old and New Testaments, basically it devotes a formal agreement between two parties binding them mutually to undertake on each other's behalf. The logically [used of relations between God and man] it devotes a gracious undertaking entered into by God for the benefit and blessing of man, and specifically of those men who by faith receive the promises and commit themselves to the obligations which this undertaking involves.

The Old Testament identifies three different types of legal relationships :

(A) A two side covenant between human parties both of which voluntarily accept the terms of agreement;

(B) A one-sided disposition imposed by a superior party; and

(C) God's self imposed obligation, for the reconciliation of sinners to himself.

As He stated to Abraham, "*I will establish my covenant between thee to be a God into thee and to thy seed after thee.*"

[Genesis 17: 7]

2. As quoted by Charles Ryrie in the Basic Theology, B. B. Warfield from the International Standard Bible Encyclopaedia.

3. A man who behaves according to the message of the Lord Jesus Christ.

4. For it, shows how God can transform man, as man can never become completely good by his own efforts.

CHAPTER-3
HINDUISM

Dedication to Equality on the Basis of the Concept of *Vasudhaiv Kutumbakam*

"Shanta Sankalpa Sumana Yathasyed,
Veetmanyugartimo Madabhimratyiyo,
Twatprasrishtam Madabhivadeta Prateeta,
Etattanyanam Prathamam Vara Vrane".

That is *"Hey Mrityon! May father Gautama- Vajashravasa of mine be peace tempered, gladful, angerless, and full of peaceful thoughts towards me as before! May he talk to me after identifying my deputation by you! This is the Ist boon that I demand out of three boons accorded by you."*

Above cited couplet in *Kathopnishadh* is capable of getting us well understand the spirit of dedication to peace and its establishment incorporated in Hindu religious community.

Hindu philosophy is one of the most ancient philosophies. It revolves around a Supreme Authority [God] who is the father of all. All are his off springs. This philosophy on this very count gives message of '*Vasudhaiv Kutumhakam*' [Family concept in relation to whole world] and through it calls upon individual, family-level, social, national and international peace. It innovates human being to adopt those all internal values [Non-violence, compassion, sacrifice, non-attachment, equality and liberty etcetera] which are essential for that. It aims at unity of whole human world and worship of God.

Before proceeding ahead on our subject of *'Hindu Philosophy and world peace'*, it is deemed apt that we should clarify a little more about nomenclature of this philosophy so that who are not very familiar with it, should not have a doubt.

◇ Nomenclature

What is known to us today as "*Hindu Philosophy*' "or" 'Hindu Faith' was not known as such in, ancient age. Its followers also did not give it this name. Actually, this name was given to it by others. Kakasaheb Kalelkar is considerably right when he says, "*We accepted the name given to us by others under compulsion as per not pondering over properly. Thereafter, we derived relief out of this nomenclature: today we feel glorified on that count.*"[1]

Today's Hindu religious order was '*Vedic*' in its preliminary days. Its development and extension made its followers to derive inspiration from other those treatises also [other than Vedas] which were of assistance in directing their day to day practices [worldly and relating to summum bonum - ultimate good]. On this very count, this above mentioned religious order later on became '*Shruti Smirti Puranakta*'. It means a religious order which is directed by *Shruti, Smirti* and *Puranas* [Epics].

Actually, *Vedas* continued to direct lives of Indians in a span of thousands of years prior to present times. *Vedas* call upon worship of Supreme Power: God or *Brahman*. God is symbol of human unity. Subsequently, *Vedic* philosophy had many branches [*Vaishesika. Nyaya, Samkhya, Yoga, Meemansa* and *Vedanta*], methods of worship and practices differed, faith in gods emerged [according to its own peculiar way] but faith and devotion unto Supreme Authority [God or *Brahman*] remained intact. It can be said that many gods and goddesses became adorable but God remained Supreme. Along with that, all the branches called upon those very eternal human values which are essential for all-sided development of man and which is practiced and accord state of peace to man.

Essence happens to be that Hindu Philosophy which was *Vedic* philosophy in its beginning. It means that what is termed today as Hindu Religious Order was actually *Vedic* Religious Order. Lokmanya Tilak has rightly and clearly said:

"Hinduism is staunch if faith exists in Vedas."

All aspects of life were considered by *Vedic* Religious Order. It has solicited human peace along with *Varna* and *Ashrama* System. As already stated, it revolves around *Brahman* (God) who is the source of peace in toto.

As the word '*Hindu*' is generally in use in human world, and not the *Vedic*, it will not be inappropriate, if we also use word '*Hindu*' in our further study.

As we have already discussed, total aim of *Vedas* and other treatises, was to direct Indian People to manage their day-to-day behaviour/activities, was that human beings must make their lives meaningful at individual, family-level, social, national and international planes in this world and in other world after death. Ambition had been towards a pleasant and ultimately peaceful life. It was for this very reason that there was reiteration of calling upon to tread above mentioned eternal values: we will describe them henceforth. As Hindu Philosophy defines also the term Religion and tells its aim, it will be quite good for us to know this definition and aim. Hindu Philosophy says:

"*Dharmo Dharyate Praja.*" Its simple derivation is that '*Dharma*' is apt only when adopted. What is to be adopted? - That which induces man to spend a pleasant life and achieve peace. What will ensure obtainment of pleasure and peace? This will emerge from behavioural activities which are capable of forming good character up to man and make him worthy of living such a social life which is based on equality and co-operation. Hindu philosophy says this also. It is because of religion that people live together as a unit and co-operate with each other. This is the process which ultimately leads to the state of peace. Grandfather of Hindu Philosophy *Manu* named such ten good conducts as '*Dashkam Dharmalakshanam*'. These conducts really develop humanity gradually and are absolutely necessary for peace. He said:

"Dhrati Kshama Dama Asteya Shauchamindriyanigraha
Dhee Vidya Satyakrodho Dashkam Dharma Lakshanam" [2]

Shrimad Bhagavad-Gita, which is taken to be abridged content of *Vedas*, describes twenty seven good conducts which, if practised; accord pleasure and peace to man not only in this world but even up to summon bonum. *Gita* also calls upon to be away from such conducts which are non-welfaristic. These pure conducts and non-welfaristic practices have been placed in Appendix at the end of this study.

Above mentioned discussion clears that religious faith incoporates such conducts, through which man gets developed, that brings welfare of whole dimension and ensures social progress. It is for this reason that *Dharma* is related to act of *Dharan*-that is adoption. Good conducts are to be reiterated: such a conduct must be there which should equally guide towards pleasure and welfare of all. This is the '*Religious faith*' related definition of Hindu philosophy: we can alternatively say that this is what it means by religious faith.

As this philosophy describes social cooperation to be the ground of religious faith, it is synthesising in this form. Good conduct is essential for an act of synthesis and it is in this perspective that this should be viewed. This very philosophy states:

"Dharnat Dharmam iti Aad"

Clearly, Hindu Philosophy ultimately calls upon its followers to practice in life all the human values. These conducts are very necessary for progress, prosperity, pleasure and peace. As such Hindu Philosophy is an integral part of religion. This philosophy keeps peace at top and keeps all other forms of pleasure at lower edge. It calls upon human being that he must make welfare be the ground of his all practices and actions. It prescribes that one should consider one's interest akin to other's interest. One should not aspire to do to others what he does not cherish for self. Ultimately, it is collective progress imbibed with prosperity, that is capable of really bringing state of peace and it is the motive of human life. *Mahabharata* clearly states in this context that what you do not cherish for yourself, never want that unto others. What you wish for yourself for a long time : wish that for others also. This is essence of religion know it with full caution.[3]

This also stipulates that it is duty of each one to act with spirit of all-welfare to achieve the ambition of pleasure, prosperity and peace. *Vaishesika*, a branch of Hindu Philosophy, admits peace to be the grand aim of humanity and takes it to be the basis of religion. It emphasises that there should be action for pleasure of all on equality basis. The essence is that Hindu Philosophy is dedicated to world peace.

Now, we shall describe some very important things which call upon man in Hindu Philosophy towards establishment of peace in world:

◊ A. Ekeshwarwaad

As already enunciated, the followers of Hindu Philosophy worship many gods and goddesses with vivid rituals but ultimately believe in one God. God had been accorded many names including that of *Brahman* and He has been accepted to be Supreme. He is father of all and all are His off springs. He unites all and keeps record of good and bad actions of each one. He is Chief Justice and sets punishment or reward in accordance with bad or good actions. God likes that man must conduct himself in a good way. He also likes that there should remain total unity unto all his off springs. He wants all to progress and gain peace.

◊ B. Social Cooperation and Unity

Hindu Philosophy accepts all human beings as members of one family while believing in *Ekeshwarwaad.* It is on this accord that there is faith in '*Vasudhaiv Kutumbakam*' which means that all persons on this earth are members of one family. As all happen to be the off springs of one God and all worship him, all should be cooperative to each other. This is the way to welfare. This will lead to progress. This will be instrumental in establishment of peace. Not only this, Hindu Philosophy calls upon to struggle with those who oppose this spirit of cooperation which is essential for peace establishment. Such a struggle has been termed "*humanistic*" in *Gita.*[4]

◇ C. Equality

Hindu Philosophy in its real and basic form accords everyone a right to live in accordance with one's will but this life must be based on mutual cooperation so as to establish peace feasibly in the world. An example of limit of equality: If father keeps faith in *Dwaitism* in house and son believes in one God: both can reside together cordially without any animosity. Hindu Philosophy clearly stipulates it. Father and son behave respecting sentiments and faith of each other. Not only that, if husband is a *Shaiva* [worshipper of Lord Shiva] and wife *Vaishnava* [worshipper of lord Vishnu] in this philosophy, both can spend whole life with love and cooperation. It is not essential in this philosophy that a teacher and his disciples should have single faith or single god or goddess for worship. Janardan Swami was very famous saint of *Maharashtra.* He was worshipper of Lord Shiva. His great disciple Eknath was devotee of Lord Krishna. Both had mutual regard of highest order for each other.

Lord Krishna himself clearly says in above mentioned context; "*I accept all my devotees with equal affection while I happen to be in Brahman form. They may choose mode of devotion but ultimately they tread the path told by me*"[5] what is the path? It is finally to achieve peace. It has also been named Salvation.

Vedic Rishis clearly said, "*We must tread the way and do actions that are apt.*" Lord Krishna told Arjuna in *Gita*:

"*Listen to respectfully and headedly what I say, ponder over it and imitate which you think to be proper.*"

Shrimad Bhagavad-Gita imparts a remarkable message of world-peace and it reminds people of duties through non-violence. These duties subsist equality because they are incorporated with spirit of all-sided welfare of man.

◊ D. Foremostness of Eternal Human Values

Hindu Philosophy calls upon to conduct in accordance with eternal values [amongst these non-violence, compassion, sacrifice, pity, love, nonattachment, truthfulness, cooperation, liberality etcetera are the main]. These values are permanently there in human heart and these indicate spirit of humanity. It is also the basis of religion. On this very accord, Hindu philosophy enunciates that religion is related to heart. This is reality and we must accept it. We should not expect from others what we do not think heartily apt unto self. We must, understand those eternal religious words which have been given in religious books. However, we must do it in real sense and with purity of heart. We shall be religious only while conducting so. We should definitely know that whichever may be the religious book of Hindu Philosophy [*Mahabharata, Vedas or Shrimad Bhagavad-Gita*]; each one prescribes immortal principle of world - peace to be the ground. A treatise incorporates thus for unity:

"*Let your heart, mind and objectives etc. be one, then only you will be able to be prosperous and only then you all shall be able to live with peace. Your supper, drink and works should be collective; God has assigned duties to you all at one time [age]. Let your thoughts be similar like sacrificial fire of consciousness tendency as is spoken by nave. Tread way of life together and all of you speak with unanimous voice...*"[6]

Not only in relation to unity, Hindu Philosophy calls upon in relation to other eternal values also as already mentioned earlier. Another example from *Mahabharata* in this context:

"Ashima Satyamasteyam Shauchamindriya Nigraha, Ehem Samasikam Dharma Chatuvarnayen abraveet Manu"

It means: It is every man's duty in precise to adopt cleanliness, truthfulness, honesty and non-violence while treading way to journey of life and abdicate dubious ways... as such declares *Prajati*, father *Manu*.

There are so many innumerable examples pertaining to truthfulness, Man has been called upon at every step not to give up truthfulness at all under any circumstance in his every work, thought or behavioural conduct.

There is one more citation from *Mahabharata*:

"Satyam bruyat priyam bruyat,
Na bruyat satyampriyam
Priyam cha na annritan bruyat,
Esha dharam sanatana"

It means, "*Speak but only truth and that must be sweet. It should be full of grandeur and should give peace. It must be impressive to intellect of one who hears it. It should not be said with curtness to make it cause perplexity or something like fretfulness. It should not deviate from its intent and thus abstain from being instrumental to doomness. Never speak non-truthfully, bitterly or bluntly.*"

Above mentioned are significant things which render Hindu Philosophy to be agreeable to humanity. They clarify the way to man's pleasure and prosperity so as to enable man to associate himself with formation of the state of peace from individualistic plane to international level.

As stated, Hindu Philosophy accords message of human unity while accepting God as its basis. Its principle is '*Vasudhaiv Kutumbakam*'. It is at the same time dedicated to equality and also to spirit of cooperation... more than that, it innovates human being to tread all those eternal human values which are essential; to gain the ambition of life. What ambition? It is peace in the whole world. Consecutively and, as such; Hindu Philosophy is dedicated to it.

Reference

1. *Yuganukul Hindu Jeevandrishti.*
2. *Manusmriti.*
3. *"Do not do others what ye do not wish (to be), Do to yourself; and wish for others too, what ye desire and long for yourself; this is the whole of Dharma. Heed it well."*
4. Manly.
5. *Shrimad Bhagavad-Gita.*
6. *"Your hearts, minds and object may all these be one, so shall you prosper all, and live in peace; in common be your food and drink and works; God harness you all to the same yoke; the sacrificial fire of spirit tend, ye all with one intent, as spoke the nave, walk ye together on the path of life, and speak ye all with voice unanimous, and may your mind all know the self same truth."*

■■■

CHAPTER-4
ISLAM

Adoption of Right Course under the Guidance of God for Friendship and Co-operation with All

World peace or peace in real sense of the term which covers individual as well as society and nations, says that Islam, can be achieved 'only when the mankind adopts the right course under the guidance of their Creator. The world is composed of nations, and nations are made of social groups and these social groups are nothing but combination of individuals. Hence, unless there is peace at the grassroot level, we can't think of world peace.

For individual peace, we have to determine status of man in the universe. Is he scot-free phenomenon, having no obligations, responsibility and accountability or otherwise?

Further, man is neither only material being nor spiritual, rather a combination of both. For the sake of his spiritual requirements as well as proper utilisation of meterial life, he needs some principles and guidance. He is faced with certain questions and his success depends on their correct reply; such as his status in the universe, his aim and objective, his relation with the Creator. Is he accountable for his deeds? If the game is over on the death of individual or he will face a day of judgement for his commissions and omissions etc. These pertinent questions determine the Course of life of individuals, societies and ultimately of the nations.

Philosophers and thinkers in all ages have tried their level best to answer these questions but no perfect answer is possible as man cannot overcome his limitations. Hence humanity needs guidance from the creator which is revealed by his messengers or prophets.

The holy *Qur'an*, according to Islamic faith, is one such revelation sent to the mankind through his prophet Muhammad. Before him, prophets have come in different parts of the world with divine guidance. The holy *Qur'an* and prophet Muhammad being the last link of the chain, it is all comprehensive and complete to guide the human destiny till the last day. It guides the individual in spiritual sphere, personal character and self responsibility as well as the nation in all spheres including socio-economic, political and other matters. The ultimate result of this in turn gives the individual as well to the society and nations complete security, peace and social justice.

There are only two natural foundations for raising the edifice of peace and progress, friendship and co-operation between different peoples and nations. They create a twin relationship between human beings... that of the one Lord and one father for all of them and consequently, an equality of status between all human beings. Oneness of God is the spiritual principle of human equality just as a common lineage of the high and the low, the white and the coloured races places them on the same plane of humanity. The *Qur'an* refers to the unity of human origin in the word:

"*O Mankind! We created you from a single pair of male and female, and made you into nations and tribes, that you may know each other. Surely the most honoured of you in the sight of God is he who is the most righteous of you.*"[1]

The same truth about human origin was explained by the prophet Muhammad at the time of the victory of Makka. He said:

"*Thanks are to God who has removed from you the evil and pride of ignorance. O People! All human beings are divided in two groups only: the one good and pious, who are honoured in the eyes of God, and the other licentious and evil who are contemptible in the eyes of God; otherwise all men are children of Adam, and Adam was created by God from the dust.*"

Again, on the occasion of farewell pilgrimage, he said, "*0 people! Beware! Your Lord is one. There is no superiority of an Arab over a non-Arab or of a white over a black or of a black over a white, but for his piety. The most honoured among you in the sight of God is one who is most righteous.*"

According to another report he also said:

"*You are all children of Adam, and Adam was created from dust. O people! Leave pride of your ancestry, otherwise you will be lowlier that the meanest of worms in the sight of God.*"

This philosophy of life permanently establishes the unity and oneness of humanity.

Undoubtedly, it is humanism, the concept of equality of mankind, which is the real solvent of all differences based on regions, community, race, caste, sex or place of birth. Humanism recognises that all human beings have the same rights and responsibilities. Recognition of the dignity of the individual is also the basic principle of world peace. Humanism aims at spreading affection and mutual respect between all human beings, irrespective of community, caste, race or nation, to which they belong. The *Qur'an* emphasises this spirit of toleration in different ways:

"*For each we appointed a divine law and traced-out a way. Had Allah willed He could have made you one community? But that He may try you by that which He has given you [He has made you as you are]. So vie with one another in good works, unto Allah ye will all return.*"[2]

"*And if thy Lord willed, all who are on the earth would have believed together. Wouldst thou compete men until they are believers* ?"[3]

The world was, however, not in a frame of mind to pay heed to the message of equality of human beings when it was first announced by the Prophet of Islam. It was then a racial call making a clean sweep of the then social relationships and economic and political orders. So striking and revolutionary was the message that it had sent the world into jitters. Today we find the principle of human equality enshrined in the constitution of different countries and being proclaimed from the forum of the United Nations but it was all due to pioneering efforts of those who set shining examples of human equality and brotherhood at the time when they possessed the means to occupy a privileged position. It was a model established through toil and tears that later on came to be accepted as the standard for peaceful human existence in this world.

There was a time when humanity was divided into different castes and classes with varying rights and privileges. Some people considered themselves to be the sons of God. The *Pharaohs* of Egypt claimed themselves to be the incarnations of sun god while in other countries several ruling families which arrogated themselves as the progeny of the sun or the moon. The Emperors of Iran called themselves *Kasra* of *Chosroes* which meant that Divine blood flowed in their veins; the rulers of a country deemed themselves to be sons of Heaven, for they believed that the - God, with Heavens the spouse of the Goddess Earth, had given birth to the human beings among whom the *Pau Ku*, the Emperor, was the first born son of Heaven enjoying supernatural powers. The Arabs were so proud of themselves that they called the other nations of the world as '*ajamees*' or the dumps. Divine right of kingship was a fact acknowledged all over the world. But this was not all; another class of *ecclesiastics* had a dominion over everything spiritual which entitled it to special rights and privileges. The members of this class acted as the intermediaries between man and his Gods and thus were deemed entitled to receive respect of all. More often than not these men were drawn from a particular clan or family which was considered as holy and consecrated by virtue of its being associated with the gods. These two groups were jointly exploiting the masses who deemed themselves to have been created for serving these men '*chosen*' by God. An Islamic scholar says:

"*How was this concept of human equality translated into the life of men? It would be sufficient to give here just one example of it. Many of us know about the French philosopher J.J. Rousseau [1712-1778] whose famous dictum: Man is born free but everywhere he is in chains, has earned an everlasting fame for him. But few people know that when the son of Amr bin-al-Aas, the conqueror and governor of Egypt beat an Egyptian Christian and latter complained to Caliph Umar, he summoned both the governor and his son to Medina. He gave a whip to the Egyptian to beat the son of Amr as he had beaten him, and said to his governor*:

"*Whence have you made slaves of these men who had been born free of their mothers?" It ought to be remembered that these memorable words were uttered by the conqueror of Byzantine and Iranian empires more than a thousand years before Rousseau. The impact of this call of brotherhood of mankind was a greater consequence than any corresponding call in history. Muslims all over the world became race-and-colour blind making it possible for a man belonging to one nationality and ethnic stock to live in complete peace in another country and even rise to the highest position if he possessed the necessary talents.*" Throwing light on this feature of Muslim history Abd-al-Rahman Azzam said that all were equal under the triumphant monarch, who was supreme over all. And those who through talent or proper attributes climbed the ladder of rank were loyal to the monarch, not to the race or the nation. Thus you find the Persian *Barmakides*[4] and *Tahirities*[5] occupying the highest positions during the caliphate of the Arabian *Hashimates* [*Abbasids*]; so did the *Kaprolu* family[6], which came from the Albanian highlands during the Caliphate of the *Ottoman Turks*. More slaves have climbed this ladder, than their numerical proportions would indicate. *Dozens* of *Mamluks*[7] reached the height of power in Islamic states stretching from Egypt to India; they have been immortalized in monuments in Delhi and Cairo; and throughout that great Islamic territory from Atlantic to the Pacific. People did not ask about race of origin but about deeds character and religiousness. Among the *Mamluks* who attained the highest state positions we find Armenian, Russian, Sicilian, Georgian, Ciracassian, Tartar, Turks, Franks, Sudanese and Ethiopian. If we trace their pedigrees, we would discover that they represented all the colours of mankind.

The importance of this Islamic achievement is underlined by the history of last two hundred years when Europe had several times drowned itself in its blood as a result of wars aimed at regulating boundaries for the sake of ethnic minorities... wars between the French and Germans and Slave, and the Austrians; wars between the Balkan states; Russia and her neighbours; the Czechs and the Poles and the Magyars and Romanians. These differences have not subsided but increased the strife between different people in proportion to the intensity of racism and nationalism. The great worth of this accomplishment of Islam has been acknowledged by A. I. Toynbee, the noted historian philosopher of this century, in these words:

"*The extinction of race consciousness among Muslims is one of the outstanding achievements of Islam, and in the contemporary world there is, as it happens, a crying need for the propagation of this Islamic virtue... Though in certain other respects the triumph of the English speaking people may be judged, in retrospect, to have been a blessing to mankind, in this perilous matter of race feeling it can hardly be denied that it has been a misfortune.*"

◊ FUNDAMENTAL HUMAN RIGHT

Closely related with the common origin and unity of mankind are human rights which in Islam are not restricted by geographical boundaries, race or nation, but are universal in nature and enjoyed by all human beings. According to the Jurist of Islam these human rights are to be observed and respected under all circumstances, whether it is peace or war. The purpose of universal human rights being maintenance and protection of basic freedom of the individual, they assume a special importance in the preservation of world peace. In fact, no concept of international peace can be valid unless it envisages freedom, equality and justice to all human beings.

◇ The Right of Life

The sacrosanct human life cannot be taken without justification as, for example, murder, causing rebellion or disorder etc. There are numerous verses in the Qur'an viz. 4:29, 6:151 and 17:33, which forbid taking of life. It even declares that "*whatsoever kills a human being for other than manslaughter or corruption on earth, it shall be as if he had brought life to all mankind and who brings life to one, it shall be as if he had brought life to all mankind.*"[8]

◇ PROTECTION OF PROPERTY AND HONOUR

The *Qur'an* says, "*Do not eat up others property by unjust means.*"[9] As for the honour of others, it ordains, "*You who believe, do not let one (set of people) make fun of another [set], perhaps. They are not better than themselves... nor should you defame yourselves, nor insult one another by using sicknesses; it is bad to use an evil name after [entering the] faith of Islam.*"[10] The Prophet of Islam, in his last pilgrimage, told the people in his sermon:

"*Most surely, your life, your property and your honour are as sacred as this day of pilgrimage... their lives and their properties are sacred to us except when they violate the sanctity of life and property of others, and Allah alone is the judge of intentions.*"

◇ FREEDOM OF CONSCIENCE

Every individual is free to believe and practice any faith or religious community. There is no compulsion in faith[11] declares the *Qur'an* and follows it up by saying, "*Unto you, your religion, and unto me my religion.*"[12]

The prophet of Islam was told by God that "*if they turn away, we have sent you as a guard over them. Your duty is but to convey the message.*"[13]

The tolerance of other religions shown by the holy Prophet and his immediate successors have always lighted the path of Muslim nations in a way that a European writer says, "*The nobility and broad tolerance of this creed, which accepts as God-inspired all the real religions of the world, will always be a glorious heritage for mankind. On it could indeed be built a perfect world religion.*"

The followers of Islam have even been instructed not to use insulting language in regard to the creeds or the leaders or the objects of worship of the non-Muslims: The *Qur'an* says:

"*Do not abuse those whom they invoke besides Allah lest they should, in their ignorance, abuse Allah.*"[14]

And again: "*O Prophet! Invite to the way of your Lord with wisdom and excellent admonition and... Discuss things with people in the best manner. Your Lord knows best who has gone astray from His way and He knows best who is rightly guided.*"[15]

◊ Freedom of Speech and Right to Dissent

Islam places no restriction on freedom of speech and right to dissent on any matter save those which amount to disobedience of God. The prophet encouraged free discussion and at times sought the opinion of his companions on different matters. He once said:

"*My personal opinion pertaining to all worldly matters should be taken in that light and the people have the right to discuss their worldly affairs and to treat them as directed by their experience and knowledge; in some cases it may be that they have more knowledge than myself; and the matters which lslam commissioned by Allah to transmit to the people are beyond any doubt, confined to religious affair relating to belief and the law of Islam*." And he also declared, "*I am but a human being. Whenever I order you concerning some religious matter, then obey me. But whenever I tell you my opinion then I am only a human being, and you know better about your worldly affairs*."

In his first speech delivered after assuming the charge of Caliphate, Abu Bakr said:

"*O People! I have been made your ruler although I am not the best among you. If I act justly, help me; if I commit a mistake, admonish me; to be truthful means trustworthiness and falsehood amounts to swindling. Who ever is weak among you is strong in my sight until I restore his right and the strong amongst you is weak in my sight until I force him to discharge his obligation to others. Of a fact, the people are debased when they cease striving in the way of God, and they are made to face difficulties when they' adopt the ways, lewd and obscene. Obey me so long as I betake by the path shown by Allah and if I defy Allah and his Apostle, it would no longer be incumbent on- you to take orders from me*."

There are many more instances when powerful rulers were fearlessly admonished by the common people but paucity of space would not permit such incidents to be cited here. However, it would suffice to mention here that *Abu Dharr Ghiffari*, a companion of the Prophet protested vehemently when *Muawiyah*, the governor of Syria, and later on Caliph, built the first ever kingly '*Green Palace*' for himself. Abu Dharr Ghiffari criticised Muawiyah saying that if the palace was built with the latter's own income then it was wasteful extravagance, and if it was built with government money then it was criminal misappropriation of public funds as well as departure from the life-pattern of earlier caliphs.

◊ Freedom to Work

"Never has one of you eaten better food, than that which he has earned with his own hands" said the holy Prophet emphasising the importance of work. The *Qur'an* says, *"It is He who made the earth manageable for you, so walk through its track and eat of its provisions."*[16]

Islam recognises man's right to do any lawful work and to adopt any profession he likes. It places no barrier on grounds of race, colour or creed in matters of service or profession and gives complete liberty to every individual to take up any lawful work. It regards all kinds of labour, physical or mental, as honourable and respectable. In fact, Islam gave real dignity and respect to manual labour and completely abolished all distinctions between man and man on the basis of one's work.

Once the Prophet said, *"Allah has not sent a Prophet who did not work as a shepherd."* The biographies of the revered companions of the Prophet were drawn from different walks of life: Caliph Abu Bakr sold cloth as a hawker while Caliph Ali often worked in the field of Jews as casual labour.

◊ The Right to Basic Needs

Every individual is entitled to have minimum basic requirements of his family. This is one of the fundamental rights of every individual.

The principle is clarified by the holy Prophet Who said, "*Allah had made zakat obligatory upon Muslims. It is to be collected from the wealthy among you and distributed among the needy ones.*" The Prophet also said, "*The Government is the guardian of anyone who has no other guardian.*" The *Qur'an* places as much importance to the need of spending in the way of God, as to the offering of daily prayers. The Prophet is also on record that: "*If anyone dies while he owes a debt and does not leave behind any property for its payment, then responsibility for its payment is mine [as Head of the State]. But if anyone leaves any property behind, [the responsibility devolves upon] his inheritors.*" *And further, "When anyone dies in debt or leaves behind dependents that are in danger of becoming destitute, the latter should come to me because I am their guardian.*"

◊ Right to Equality before Law

Islam accords equal rights on all, irrespective of one's race, caste, colour, nationality or sex. It also does not differentiate between a Muslim and non-Muslim. Both enjoy equal civil rights and the same civil and criminal law applies to them, except that in their personal and religious matters each is to be governed by the law of his own religious community. An Islamic State has no right to interfere in the personal or religious laws of non Muslims nor can it apply Muslim personal law on them.

Another important point with regard to equality before law is that Islam makes no difference between the ruling classes and the ordinary citizens or between the rich and the poor or for the matter, between any priestly class and the common man in respect of law. The same law applies to all citizens, irrespective of their social or political status. The holy Prophet offers before his death, his own self for the satisfaction of any claim that anyone might have against him. When he was once approached to remit the punishment prescribed by the law of God, the Prophet angrily replied, "*I swear by Allah that if Fatimah, daughter of Muhammad, should steal, I would have her hand cut off.*" Likewise, Umar, the second Caliph, forced Jabalah bin Aiham, the ruler of native State, to satisfy the claim of common man against him. Umar also turned down the request for legal safeguards against the governors of different countries appointed by him.

◊ The Right to Private Property

While Islam lays emphasis on earning one's livelihood through lawful means[17] and sharing one's earnings with the poor and the needy.[18] It recognises the individual's right to acquire and own property. It allows him to earn as much wealth as he can through his knowledge, skill and effort but does not favour expenditure on luxuries or ostentatious way of life. Islam condemns both prodigality and miserliness and recommends moderation in living.

◊ Right to Privacy

There is yet another right to an individual recognised by Islam. It allows every man to enjoy his life in privacy in his own house. The *Qur'an* says, "*You who believe, do not enter any house but your own unless you are sure of their occupants consent and greet them politely.*"[19]

In order to preserve the, sanctity of this right, it further advises, "*Do not spy on one another, nor let any of you backbite others. Would one of you like to eat his dead brother's flesh? You would loath it! Heed Allah, for Allah is of-Returning, Merciful.*"[20]

◊ PLEADGES, PACTS AND TREATIES

Islamic teachings and the practice of the Prophet base international relations on the concept that the people of the world are:

- Muslims or non-Muslim citizen of an Islamic state;
- Non- Muslims in treaty relations with Islam; or
- Non-Muslims having no treaty relations with Muslims.

Scholars have subsequently extended these concepts to cover Muslim nations with non-Muslim minorities and vice-versa. It may be mentioned here that from the very beginning it was agreed that a Muslim state may have non-Muslim citizens who constitute a nation along with the Muslim Constitution of the first Islamic state of Medina, promulgated by the Prophet, recognised the Jews and other non-Muslim residents of Medina, as constituents of the Islamic state with the same rights and duties as the Muslims. Likewise Muslims living in non-Muslim countries were duty bound to act as loyal citizens and even fight for its defence.

A precedent is provided by the companions of the holy Prophet who had migrated to Abyssinia owing to the persecution of Muslims by the Meccan oligarchy. The migrants had offered to fight in defence of Abyssinia when its security was threatened. It should also be remembered that the Muslim state has no power to interfere in the religious matters of its non-Muslim citizens and similarly Muslims are permitted by the *Shariah* to live as citizens in a non-Muslim country provided they are free to observe their religious practices and teach their faith to their children. Now, coming back to the subject under discussion, the purpose of international relations and treaties is to establish peace between people of different cultures and faiths. Peace being fundamental and basic to life in Islam... as its very name signifies an Islamic state is required to make every effort to establish and maintain peace with all countries which are willing to cooperate in achieving this objective. It is its duty to enter into friendly agreement with any country which wants to establish such relations. Respect for agreements and pacts is a fundamental principle of Islam and it does not allow Muslims to violate them.

◊ Muslim Countries

A natural consequence of their belief in Allah and their submission to His law is that Muslim countries are enjoined to maintain peaceful relations. If there is any dispute between two Muslim countries or one of them takes to aggression against the other, then other Muslim countries have a legal moral obligation to help the aggrieved against the aggressor and try to establish peace between the warring countries on equitable terms through negotiations, arbitrations and similar other methods. The *Qur'an* says, "*If two parties of believers fall to fighting then make peace betwixt them. And if one party of them does wrong to the other, fight that which does wrong until it returns to the law of Allah: then, if it returns, make peace between them justly and act equitably. Verily! Allah loves the just. The believers are but brothers. Therefore, make peace between brethren and fear Allah, that you may receive Mercy.*"[21]

◊ Non-Muslim Countries with Contractual Obligations

Islam had laid such an emphasis on the sanctity of a pledge that it even overrides the obligation of Muslim brotherhood. We read in the *Qur'an*:

"But if they [Muslim] seek help from you in the matter of religion, then it is your duty to help [them] except against the people between whom and you there is a treaty."[22] An example of how his Quaranic injunction is to be acted upon is furnished by the return of Abu Jandal by the Messenger of Allah. At Hydaybia, the Prophet agreed to a truce with the Quraish of Makka. The treaty contained a condition that if anyone from the Quraish goes over to the Muslims, he will return to Quraish of Makka. The treaty had yet to be signed when Abu Jandal, the son of Suhayl, the Qurraishite envoy negotiating the treaty, appeared in chains. He had escaped from Makka and come to the Prophet seeking asylum straggling in fetters by a rugged, rocky tract; Suhayl lost no time to demand his return. Muslims intervened to point out that the treaty had yet to be signed, but the Prophet handed over Abu Jandal back to his father Suhayl. Islam, thus, enjoins Muslims to observe their treaty obligations and universally accept code of morality and for that reason, they are not allowed to help even their oppressed Muslim brethren living in a country with which they have a treaty. Islamic *Shariah* emphasises in strongest terms the necessity to adhere to the conditions of contract made with foreign powers whether friend or foe. No matter what happens. Muslims are not allowed to break their promises unilaterally.

◊ Countries without any Treaty

Justice and equity are the two criteria laid down for dealing with all others whether there is a treaty or not. The *Qur'an* enjoins Muslims:

"O believers! Be steadfast witness for Allah in equity, and let not hatred of any people seduce you that deal not justly.

Do justice, for it is nearer to piety, and fear Allah. Help you one another in righteousness and piety. Help not one another in sin and aggression, and fear Allah."[23]

Thus the fundamental principle that governs foreign relations in Islam is that both Muslim and non-Muslims are absolutely equal and justice should regulate the relationship between them. Islam invites all to peace and instructs its followers to maintain peace with all. Says the *Qur'an*:

"*O ye who believe! All of you, into peaceful submission [unto Him] : and follow not in the footsteps of the devil: Lo he is an open enemy for you.*"[24]

The *Qur'an* asks the Muslims that:

"*And if they incline to peace, incline thou also for it, and put your trust in Allah, Lo! He is the All-Hearing, the All-knowing. And if they intend to deceive thee, then Lo! Allah is sufficient for thee.*"[25]

The *Qur'an* enjoins Muslims to keep peace and maintain cordial relations with all non-belligerent powers:

"*Allah forbidden you not, with regard to those who warred not against you on account of religion and drove you not out from your homes, from dealing kindly and justly with them Lo! Allah loveth the just dealers.*"[26]

"*So if they hold aloof from you and wage not war against you and offer you peace, Allah alloweth you no way against them.*"[27]

These verses will show that the Muslims are enjoined by God to advance the cause of peace and friendly relations betwixt different people. Even if the enemy is treacherous and not trustworthy, Muslims are asked to accept the offer of peace and leave all matters to God. And when any other nation makes an offer of peace, it becomes their bounden duty to accept it. All those verses go to show that international relations are based on goodwill and justice, seeking equality among people, irrespective of cast, colour, creed or race.

In conclusion we can say that some of the basic principles for world peace, which the *Qur'an* and Prophet Muhammad have given, are as follows:

- All human beings are members of one family having Adam and Eve as their parents;
- Different tribes and nations are not only for the sake of knowing each from other. None is by birth superior or inferior. Of course, the noblest is one who is the most righteous;
- There is no superiority or preference for any particular nation black or white, north or south, east or west all-are equals;
- Life, honour and property of all is equally respected and to be protected;
- Freedom of faith is guaranteed for all nations and individuals;
- Islam is against the supremacy of man on man, all are slaves of the Almighty alone;
- Islam is against colonialism, racialism and aggressive nationalism - which calls for 'my nation right and wrong';
- All international treaties and agreements have to be respected in letter and spirit;
- No exploitation of any individual or society is allowed; and
- Justice is the guiding principle for all human behaviours and relations;

Regarding economic equality, Islam stands for justice in this field also. Everybody should get his due share and equal opportunity in the society. The handicapped, the destitute and the down-trodden deserve special attention. It is the duty of the society and the state to take care of all such people without fail. Islam has made *Zakat* [2.1/2% of capital wealth] as well as *Ushr* [10% of agricultural products] compulsory for wealthy people which have to be distributed among needy persons. It has taken different steps to bridge the gap between the rich and the poor. Unlimited disparity and exploitation of the week is not permitted. Islam neither believes in artificial equality nor the exploitation of workers and poor.

The overall check and balance maintained in an Islamic system of life ensure justice, welfare and peace for all. Islamic principles are practicable and having evolving nature without compromise on basic principles, even today they bear fruitfulness and effectiveness.

References

1. 49:13

2. 5: 48

3. 10: 100

4. A Family of *Viziers* which flourished in 752-903 AD and became the most powerful administrators of the Empire ranking next to the Caliphs.

5. Tahir Ibn-al-Husain of *Khurasan*, descendant of a Persian slave, who became governor of all Muslim lands east of Baghdad stretching beyond the Oyus, appointed by the Caliph-al-Mamum in 820 AD.

6. Grand *Viziers* who uphold the structure and prestige of the Ottoman Empire in the late sixteenth and early 19th centuries.

7. The *Mamluks*, originally slaves brought to Egypt in the 10th century founded two dynasties in Egypt which lasted 250 years. In India also a slave dynasty ruled the country from 1206 to 1290 AD. In both these countries they checked the hitherto unrestrained barbarian Monghol hordes which had laid waste flourishing countries from the borders of China to Eastern Europe.

8. 5: 32

9. 2: 188

10. 49: 11-12

11. 2: 256

12. 109: 6

13. 42: 48

14. 6: 108

15. 16: 125

16. 67: 15

17. 2: 188

18. 51: 19

19. 24: 27

20. 49: 12

21. 49: 9-10

22. 8: 72

23. 5:2

24. 2: 208

25. 8: 61

26. 60: 8

27. 4: 90

CHAPTER-5

JAINISM

Firm Faith on Non-Violence with a Feeling of Live and Let Live

"Savvesi Jeeviam Piyam,
Panin Cha Piya Daya,
Atmavat Sarvabhuteshu,
Parasparopgriho Jeevanam,
Ahimsa Parmo Dharma"

It means – All love life; living being like piety. It is a characteristic of life that the gratifying activity is reciprocated among all; equally bearing life. Non-violence is religion in grandeur.

Above cited lines in Jain *Vangamaya* clarify that non-violence is deeply present as a vital element in relation to establishment of peace through non-violence. Whole philosophy of this religion community revolves around non-violence. We can form it so: Non-violence is central point of Jain philosophy. Jainism again and again calls upon a human being that he should carry on the journey of life on the basis of non-violence.

Non-violence is at top in Jain philosophy and, as such, a learned person aptly says, *" Life of this philosophy exists in non-violence and it is rooted in it."* Emphasis of whole Jain Philosophy is that a human being should adopt spirit of non-violence by heart and subsequently there should be an attempt to practise it to the most possible extent. It will result in pleasure, prosperity and ultimately peace, which is the goal of human life.

Now, we should proceed further in context of Jain Philosophy and universal peace. It will be apt, prior to that, to throw light precisely on non-violence.

◊ Non-violence

Analysis of *Ahimsa* comes to be A + *Himsa,* that is,

negativism of violence. It stipulates abstinence from violence. Now, the question arises as to what violence is? Jain philosophy states in this regard, "*Attack on life is violence-abstaining from this absolutely denotes non-violence.*" This is a simple meaning. In case we explain it for a while, we shall find a meaning that there still remains some duty to be filled: After we desist from causing violence on some human beings. This sprouts the element of duty, mercy, compassion, delightfulness, friendliness, favour etcetera in relation to non-violence. Non-violence in real sense appears in presence of this sproutness.

Really, non-violence is in its permanent mode that spirit which is indicative of human existence. A man gets a situation of progress and peace according to its development by him. Peace is motive of human life subsequently to progress and, as such, Jain philosophy beseeches maximum feasible development of non-violence and its pursuit consecutively. This philosophy has a credit to render probably the deepest elaboration in context of *Ahimsa* and it is very detailed also but we are not marching ahead very deeply and at very much details.

A man takes birth in this world and soon after he is involved in wordily practices. This is natural process. These practices take a human being to pleasure, prosperity and peace after that or there can be opposite to that. The opposite situation is that of grief, non prosperity and non-peacefulness. This is a simple thing. Pleasure, prosperity and peace are relevant to human life and Jain Philosophy on this accord prescribed five great orders around human practices while disciplining them through regulations. Non-violence is foremost among these five. The remaining four rotate around it.[1] Jain philosophy holds that only a human being well-incorporated with these five great orders can be welfaristic to society along with the welfare to self. He can then be vital to peace.

Four great orders in addition to non-violence are:

- TRUTH : That is separation from every form of non-truth;
- NON-THEFT : Not taking a thing, without owner's consent;
- CELIBACY : Abstinence from mating; and
- NON-ATTACHMENT : Giving up property etc. Collections relating to physical attribute.

As already illustrated, non-violence is not only foremost in above mentioned great orders; it is also basis of these all. As such, we once again approach the aspect of peace-establishment through non-violence propagated by Jain Philosophy, which fully favours universal non-violence. Life is dear to all. All have a right to live. This philosophy calls upon humanity that no one should attempt to discard this right. It has been definitely mentioned in *Acharangastura* that nothing is inaccessible as far as death is concerned. All living beings love life. They like pleasure and dislike grief. They want life and escape destruction. They cherish a long life. All love life.[2]

Right to living being bestowed unto all, there must be definiteness of this right pertaining to all. It is essential for it that all must grasp importance of dear life of each other. This is possible only through non-violent spirit, tendency and actions. This is the reason that Jain religious community considers it natural that every living being has substantial right to live and calls upon to carry out gradual development of spirit and tendencies relating to non-violence. This sect also declares non-violence to be very affectionate *BRAHMAN* for living beings along with most peace-imparting.[3]

Lord Mahavira on this very accord stated, "*A person should not kill. He should not be a cause to killing and must not ratify the killing carried out by any other.*"[4]

The philosophy of Jainism prescribes right of life for all and determines principle of universal non-violence. As such, it sets a scale of non-violence for saints' and household people. Along with that, it calls upon to practice four great orders in order to gain a surety pertaining to that. These orders are not only significant, they are very essential. A person shall be achieving pleasure and prosperity in proportion to this endeavour to promote these orders at personal, family, social, national or international planes and their practice in life. These will make him successful in sphere of establishment of world-peace. These four orders are:

- Spirit of Fraternity;
- Merrily Spirit: that is respecting others with purity at heart;
- Spirit of Compassions: it is said about it in *Sutrakritanga* [2:2:13] - even a household person should be considerate in principle towards living beings. It is incumbent on us to be honest and equal towards all [5]; and
- Mediocre Spirit: it denotes that one should become indifferent in case other one is not at all poised to accept a reality and expresses – opposite views. Such indifference must be without even an iota of malice.

Above mentioned is non-violent path and Jain religious community is determined to get world peace by treading this path. Non-violence clarifies the way to live and let live. It is full of those of all human values which are necessary for the development of humanity and without which establishment of peace is not possible. Non-violence is religion in itself and, as such, it is wholly competent in itself as far as establishment of world peace is concerned.

This is the basis of Jain Philosophy and it holds that there remains nothing to be done or to gain after non-violence in toto. This dictum is important, however, it will not be non-contextual that we should briefly know those immortal messages which Jain Philosophy prescribed for human beings to adopt in day to day practical life. This attempt is specifically with a point of view that we can purify our conduct by adopting them. This attempt shall ensure our self-progress and we shall be definitely able to march in the direction of peace. Some of the dictums are:

◊ **Aptness of life at present**

Jain Philosophy calls upon a person to gain peace, pleasure and prosperity through his or her actions in present life itself. It renders a message towards aptness of life at present and desists from imagination pertaining to another birth. It states - March towards aptness in this very life, get rid of dying and birth cycle and in order to obtain this end, do not insult anyone as it is improper action.[6]

First *Thirthankara* Rishabhdev said to his son in context of aptness of present life:

"Sabujhah Kim Na Bujhah? Sabohi Khalum Pechcha Dullaha,

Nau Huvanammati Raeeo-No Sulaham Punaravi Jeeviyam"[7]

It means, it is difficult to benefit from such sermons after this life. The days that are gone shall never be back. It is also not certain that there will be human birth again. As such, this very life must be made apt and peace should be obtained.

◊ **Self-less and disciplined life**

It is a fact that if a person or assembly of persons, society or nation or a group of nations give up spirit of selfishness, most of the problems shall perish and there will be peace in the world. It is on this accord that Jain

Philosophy emphasises non-selfishness at every step. It clearly indicates that the actions should be devoid of attachment. Why? Because, one will have to reap as per his deeds. No one will be able to... help him/her in that eventuality.[8] As such, it is required that a person should non-selfishly give up "*bad action, untruthful statements, personal property, sexual activities and those things which do not stand given to him/her voluntarily. It is because these selfish actions inflict stabs on all living beings... A prudent person is one who keeps himself/herself away from these all.*"[9]

It is incumbent on a person to grasp non-selfishness up to his nature as it is bestowed with attribute of permanence. Opposite to it, selfishness is full of non-permanence. Permanent always accords welfare whereas a temporary one is never akin to welfare. It is for this reason that a temporary spirit seems to be capturing immediate motive but it - is without truth owing to being temporary.

As such, it is only good that a human being should act for welfare of all without selfishness and this should be done after applying thought and caution. *Sutrakritanga* [4:1:14] sates:

"*Those who do not ponder over in terms of future and derive temporary pleasure only presently shall repent when their youth and vital life shall be over.*"

Jain philosophy has sent a message that a human being should live a disciplined life. Discipline is constant need of human life. One remains uncontrolled without it and creates non-peaceful atmosphere per interference in life of others. In order that a person's life should not be unrestrained and that one should not be unrestrained and that one should be in control, Jain Philosophy states,." . *He... alone is duly disciplined who protects others, who resides where others did not like to be, who is fearless and who is supported with integrated character*" [10]

Discipline has been attached with self-control in this philosophy and it has been stated:

"One who controls himself according to regulations who is praised by many others, who is not in any sort of worldly bondages, who is always like a clear lake, he alone can claim to have adopted the Kashyap rule."[11]

◊ **Equality**

As a matter of fact, there is no need of any specific elaboration or comment towards word equality as Jain religious community is totally dedicated to equality while revolving around non-violence. Even then, it will not be unfair to pursue the last significant sermons in this philosophy. It has been many a times; innumerable times reiterated in Jain Philosophy that all human beings are equal. No one can be termed as small or big. A man becomes good or bad in accordance with his actions. *Uttaradhyayan* states so conclusively:

"Anyone can be Brahmin, Kshatriya, Vaishya or Shudra as per actions."[12]

No one is great by birth; all twenty four *Tirthankaras* advised this again and again and accordingly imparted message of human equality. The last *Tirthankara* Lord Mahavira on this very accord once said:

"One who is sad bears pain again and again... . So, a clever sage must deeply think and derive that all existing living beings are like him."[13]

In this manner, Jain Philosophy inspires to think in terms of the highest form of equality among all living beings and paves way to real world peace.

The above mentioned are main sermons. Non-violence is the basis of all these sermons in Jain Philosophy and community. It is so in consideration of establishment of world peace. These sermons not only motivate but also call upon a human being that one has to adopt non-violence as it is the touch stone of live and let live principle. We shall have to keep this adopting in this world and thereafter too if we are bestowed with a will of peace.

Lord Mahavira on this very consideration in a sermon to us said:

"*Desist from wounding a living being; no matter whether the living being is static or moving one, whether that one is above or below or on ground. Moksha has been said for this very purpose... it is state of peace.*"[14]

It is absolutely essential that there should be constant awakening relating to non-violence in nature. In other words, there must be gradual development of spirit of non-violence in nature of a human being. This is what Jain Philosophy calls us to do and it definitely cleans the path to world-peace. A tendency that initiates itself from personal level and then reaches up to national level to get one rid of violent spirits and activities and which attaches one to the spirit and activities akin to favour, compassion, mercy and friendliness, is certain to accord welfare to human world. This is really the non-violent way. This is the most stout and viable way to peace establishment.

Jain Philosophy is also an ideal before us in relation to solving international problems and resultant conflicts. Practise on this ideal is really amply and ably fruitful. There is aspect of *Anekantavad* in this philosophy. According to it, non- alertness is at the root of evils in human life. As such man must never be ready to part with non-alertness and should act with alertness and cautiousness. One should admit his mistake, if any. The admittance gives birth to non-violence. Inherited non-violence should subsequently be made forceful and matured. It requires bravery. Any dispute, however big, can be resolved through it. There is a need to accept it heartily and it shall have to be accepted because as already stated, human existence is connected with it. A contemporary Jain Saint's statement in this regard is quite true. He says :

"*Human existence will depend upon non-violence. Existence of non-violence is existence of man. Human existence is only relevant as per dignity of principle of non-violence. Non-violence is essential for cooperation, co-existence, world-fraternity and ultimately for world peace. We shall have to admit that its existence is compulsory for existence of human life. One, who cherishes for human existence, should naturally wish peace for it. In absence of non-violence, a person shall become eater of other one, Violence is brutish whereas non-violence in human, and Humanity of a person demands full non-violence is human. Humanity of a person demands full non-violence unto self and thereby gaining peace through self-progress. It is also expected that he should take the world on this nice path. Lord Mahavira was bestowed with non-violence in toto. He remains, as such, lively symbol of non-violence and he has been calling upon to gain peace consequently and perpetually. Welfare of world is epitomized in this call. So, it is constant duty of man that he must adopt religion of non-violence towards gaining peace. He should subsequently bring this world also in sphere of religion of non-violence with an ambition of universal welfare. It is through this venture that he shall be able to render his contribution to and for world peace.*"

Obviously, Jain religious community is also fully dedicated to peace for each and every one in the world. It favours human conduct and practices on basis of those eternal values which are helpful in establishment of universal peace and that happens to have non- violence as central point.

References

1. All the four great orders - Truth, Non-stealing, Celibacy and Nonattachment are fully gainful in the tendency to non-violence and so happen to be its integral part.
2. "For there is nothing inaccessible -for death. All beings are fond of life, like pleasure, hate pain, and shun destruction, like life; long life happens to be their desire. To all life is dear:' [Acharangasutra, 1:2:3:4]
3. "*Ahimsa Savvasattanam sada Nivveyakarika*; *Ahimsa Savvasattesu param Banbhamanidiyam*." [Isi. 45:20, page 282]
4. 'He should not kill, or cause others to kill; not consent to the killing of other'. [Acharangastura 1:3:3:3]
5. The man who still lives in the house should in accordance with creed be merciful to living being; we are bidden to be fair and equal with all... [*Sutrakritanga* 2:2:13]
6. Sutrakritanga 2:2:2
7. It is difficult to obtain instructions in it after this life. The days [that are gone by] will never return, nor it is easy a second time to obtain human life. [Sutrakritanga 2/1/1]
8. *Sutrakritanga* 9:5
9. *Sutrakritanga* 9:10
10. He who is very well disciplined who protects others, who lives in a place removed from other people, who is not frightened by dangers, possesses right conduct...[*Sutrakritanga* 2/2/17]
11. "*A man who controls himself according to (the law), who is praised by many people and is not bound by... and worldly ties, who are always pure, like a lake proclaims the law of Kashyap...*" [*Sutrakritanga* 2:2:7]
12. "*By one's actions one becomes a Brahmin or a Kshatriya, or a Vaishya or a Shudra...*" [*Uttaradhyayan* 25:3]
13. *Sutrakritanga* 2:2:2
14. "*...should cease to injure living beings whether they move or not, on high, below and on earth. For this, has been called the 'Nirvana' which consists in peace.*" [*Sutrakritanga* 4:1:20]

CHAPTER-6
SIKHISM

Development of the Character of Courage, Readiness for Sacrifice to Protect the Weak

"IK OAMKARA"	: There is but one God [Manifested as well as unmanifested *Brahman*]
"SATNAM"	: His name is TRUTH.
"KARTA PURUKH"	: A *Pursha* who is the Creator.
"NIRBHAU"	: Without any fear.
"NIRVAIR"	: Without any enmity.
"AKAL MURAT"	: Whom Death cannot assail, self illuminated.
"AJUNI"	: Unborn.
"SAIBHAM"	: Self-existent.
"GURPRASAD"	: With the Grace of the *Guru* [Preceptor].

The above quoted lines represent the fundamental principles of the Sikh faith. All the Sikh *Gurus* have dwelt on the above in their writings. The logic of this persuasion becomes obvious by a study of the saying and composition of the Sikh *Gurus* in the *Guru Granth Saheb*.

◊ MEANING OF THE 'GURU'

The meaning of the *'Guru'* as explained by Guru Gobind Singh: *'Gu'* means inertia, nascence, and matter; *'Ru'* means the principle which illuminates the mind. *Guru* thus means the descent of divine guidance to mankind through a teacher or a divine impulsion of human conscience. All the same the connotation of the word *Guru* is still wider.

◊ GURU GRANTH SAHEB

The *Guru Granth Saheb* is the visible form of the invisible *Guru* and is held in deep reverence. It extols self-abrogation and renunciation and attendant virtues, mercy, generosity, restraint and simplicity. It highlights to renounce passions and subdue the senses. The *Guru Granth Saheb* contains sublime truth, proclaims God, lays stress on mediation on true one, and lays down moral and ethical rules for development of soul, spiritual salvation and unity with God. The *Guru Granth Saheb* is secular in character and cosmopolitan in nature, The *Granth Saheb* speaks of one True God, fearless and devoid of enmity, omnipotent and omniscient. The Granth Saheb provides cohesion and ensures unity by checking fissiparous tendencies among the mankind. The *Guru Granth Saheb* has a significant unifying and emotionally integrating factor, which generates a strong spirit of cooperation and solidarity in thought. The *Granth Saheb* describes the cosmic principles which pervade the universe and in it are enshrined the teachings and essentials of Sikhism. The *Guru Granth Saheb* gives the message of unity and expects a Sikh to eschew pride and practice humility.

"*One father*; *we the Children of one God,*" this is the clarion call which runs through the pages of the *Granth Saheb*. The inalienable Creator of the Universe has taken on Himself to provide for our daily needs then why should we worry and fight among ourselves?

Saint Kabir has said:

"*First was created the light of Allah;*

Human beings were created through nature.

The whole world has been created from the primordial light;

Who good, who bad?"[1]

The feeling of '*mine and thine*' and all quarrels originate from the notion of good and bad. According to *Gurubani*, this feeling has its root in the human instinct of '*ego'*. This gives rise to the '*sense of personality*' within us. This has been given the compendious name: "*Haumain*", which in common parlance means sense, of ego, but '*Gurubani*' [Sayings and compositions of Sikh *Gurus*] has dealt with this at length. The pace was set by Guru Nanak, who after discussing this primary instinct came to the conclusion:

"*Haumain is a deep seated malady; specific remedy is also within it.*"[2]

This, in fact, means that by working within the four corners of our personality, we have to work our way up to attain salvation. There is no room here within the limits of this brief discourse to dilate on the Sikh religious philosophy to unfold the mysteries of human mind and explain the truth about human activity and the instincts that lie behind it. However, we wish to give here the phenomenon of change in human behaviour in our country throughout the ages as enunciated in Sikh scripture:

- In Satyug, everybody was contended; *Dharama* on all its four feet was attended to;
- They sang the praise to *Hari* [God] from the core of their heart;
- Enjoyed the highest comforts every heart sang the praises of God;
- In their souls and outside they saw *Hari/Prabhu* [God] and none else;
- They mediated on one God and God came to their help; they were honoured in the eyes of God;
- *Tretayug* came, emphasis was on physical strength, for that they practised celibacy and discipline;
- The fourth feet collapsed, life rested on three legs, in their minds they burned with rage;
- Inside, they had poisonous anger; the rulers attacked and fought each other and suffered;

- Inside they had the malady of egoism and arrogance;
- God was kind; this poison could be removed by God's name;
- *Duaperyug* came, dualism prevailed, *Gopies* and *Krishna* were created;
- They [the people] had recourse to penances and practiced charity and other rituals;
- Ritualism prevailed and *Dharma* now rested on two legs;
- Many warriors were born; they burned with pride of ego;
- But God was kind. *Gurus* and *Sadhus* met to wash away sins;
- *Hari* [God] created *Kaliyug*[3] three feet of *Dharma* collapsed, it now rested on one leg;
- Work hard on *Guru's* commandments, this was the remedy prescribed by God, praise be for God and attain peace; and
- This is the season for God's name; harvest of *'Na' 'am'* is the yield.[4]

This was the transformation enunciated in the idiom of religion.

Having arrived at this stage of development, let us now pick up the thread of Guru Nanak's age, who was the most remarkable personality of his age. His analysis of the situation around was very clear.

According to Guru Nanak, the ills of the age could be ascribed to the acquisitive instinct dominating the minds of the rulers:

"*The ruler is never satiated with his territorial possessions*;

"*Who has filled to the full the oceans* ?"[5]

This one line dictum was the key for understanding the turmoil and sufferings of the age. The rulers were by nature aggressive and annexationist. They made wars for personal aggrandisement. The Guru says that just as the ocean is full of limitless water, but its thirst for more and more water is never quenched even though the rivers and streams rush into it to get absorbed in the limitless expanse of water.

This, of course, was the primary cause of turmoil, wars, death and destruction, but there was another equally important cause and the divisions and barriers created by man not only among the various people; but also within each society. This generated enmities not only among various territorial states but also within each society. This generated enmities not only among various territorial states but also within different societies. War, conflicts, bloodshed was the order of the day. While repeatedly reminding about the brotherhood of man on account of the common origin of mankind, Guru Nanak could not shut his eyes to the ills from which his own country suffered. They say charity begins at home: It is no use pontificating to the world about the highest ideals, when our own house is on fire. Incidentally, the situation prevailing in our country in those days was applicable to other countries also and seeds of internal and external conflicts were present in every country; hence the frequency of fighting among the peoples. This is what Guru Nanak had to say about this state of affairs:

- The generous people sinned in order to practice generosity;
- The *Gurus* went to the homes of their disciples to instruct them;
- The wife cared for her husband only for money; Otherwise they went and wandered anywh[illegible],

- None cared for the *Vedas* and *Shastras*; [6]
- They cared for their own worship;
- The *Qazis* had sessions for dealing out justice;
- They counted their beads in the name of God;
- They took bribe and trampled under foot the legal rights; If anyone questioned, they quoted from the book [Qur'an]; *Turk Mantra* [*Quaranic Qalma*] was in their mind;
- They plunged the people and took bribes.[7]

So much for the system prevailing in those days, the above is not a solitary example to show that the Sikh Gurus censured the justice of the *Qazis*; the Sikh *Gurus* frequently referred to the capricious nature of the *Qazis* as a class and their oppressive proclivities. Lack of space does not allow us to quote from the *Gurus*, but we cannot avoid giving here a brief account of the political life of those days:

"*Think! The symptoms of Kaliyug; recognition is for those who use force to gain their ends* :

A. "*If anyone stands by truth, he is ruined, no penance in penance homes*;

"*If anyone names the wrongdoers, he gets bad name, these are the symptoms of Kaliyug*;

"*The Sikdars*[8] *often come to the grief; how the subordinates will fear them*;

"*When the Sikdars are bound in chains, they die at the hands of their own servants*."[9]

B. '*The deer, the eagles and Sikdars have learnt, this*;

"*Net is spread; they help catch their own kind*;[10]

"They have no place in future;

"He is pandit;[11] *he is a wise expert, who remembers God*;

"First the root grows inside earth, and then it grows up to provide shade."

C. *"Rulers the lions, muqaddams, the dogs*;[12]

"The subordinates wounded their claws;

"The blood was licked by dogs;

"Where the souls have to render their account;

"There their noses will be cut and declared unreliable backbiters."[13]

These are only samples to show that the *Gurus* were fully conscious and wide awake about the political system prevailing in the country. They were men of the world and had not turned recluse to undergo penance for their salvation. They worked and made sacrifices for the salvation of people. For the salvation of the soul, they believed in the liberation of man. They criticised and even condemned those saints who had renounced the world and were closely ensconced in mountain retreats. The Sikh *Gurus* lived, worked, fought and made sacrifices in the arena of society.

After centuries of suffering of the people Guru Nanak appeared on the scene to offer a clear analysis of the situation prevailing at that time and provide remedies. He also suggested that the people would have to fight for their liberation.

The society in our country can be taken as an archetype for all other societies of the world. The nature of the society made for the disturbed state both within and outside the borders of every country. Disturbances were frequent and peace was so rare that the people were thirsting for a settled life even for a brief period.

The wise men in our country had taken to a scheduled life of dedication in the far off mountains. They had set their face against the world. Pretenders were organised in various saintly orders and enjoyed a parasitical living. They exacted their dues from the people as harshly as the government collectors did. The people were ground down by these exactions. A crude system of checks and balances prevailed. The people frequently had recourse to armed rebellion against established authority. The disturbances frequently spilled over to the neighbouring lands. In our country incursions, raids and invasions from the North-West were frequent and the suffering of the people living in Punjab, Delhi and other border lands was beyond description. *Guru Nanak* saw with his own eyes the death and destruction following Babar's invasion of Eminabad in 1521. This is what Guru Nanak had to say on that occasion:

"*Mughals and Pathans fought each other; Swords were used in the battlefield*;

"*They took aim and shot with their guns; and*

"*They stormed with their elephants.*"[14]

This was the inexorable repetition of history; carnage of this nature had been taking place from the earliest times. Guru Nanak put the history and politics of our country in proper perspective:

"*Khurasan was owned up*;[15]

"*Hindustan was put to fright*;

"*God does not accept any blame; He made the Mughals to invade.*"[16]

Guru Nanak here interprets history and politics correctly by saying that the raids from the north-west did not arise from Hindu-Muslim antagonism, but this has been the normal cause of our history. In giving a graphic account of the suffering from Babar's invasions and the oppression by Babar's Begs, he was meticulous in showing the impact equally upon the Hindus and Muslims and the womenfolk matter in the least. Incidentally, *Guru Nanak* was even-handed in giving instruction or criticising the Hindu and Muslim faiths. *Gurubani* is replete with references to Hindu texts; Hindu tenets and Hindu practices, but apt references to Muslim faith have also been made:

- Kindness the mosque, devotion the prayer mat, Qur'an the sense of justness;
- Modesty the circumcision, good bearing the fast, be a Muslim;
- Good deeds the '*Ka' aba*', [17] truths the *Pir*, generosity the *Kalma* and *Namaz*;
- Rosary the peace loving habits, 0 Nanak! He will protect honour.[18]
- Five times the *Namaz* they have distinct names of their own;[19]
- First, the truth, honest deeds the second, third goodwill for all;
- Fourth good intentions; fifth praise of God;

  Good deeds the *Kalma*;[20] then deserve to be Muslim.[21]
- It is difficult to be called a *Mohammedan*; if one is, let him be known a *Mohammedan*;
- First, he should accept the faith of Muslim saints;
- Then he should give away in charity to rinse out the rust;[22]
- Be determined to make the faith your path-indicator;
- Remove the misconception of life and death;

- He should bow to God's will, accept the Creator and obliterate himself;
- O Nanak! He should be merciful to all beings; then he deserves to be called a *Mohammedan*.
- All the twenty-four hours, he is wandering for his appetite;
- How he should avoid hell he has no mind for the *Rasul* [Prophet] [23].

So much for the *Mohammedans*; but *Guru Nanak* was unsparing in his criticism of the Hindus. First, he condemned the inhuman caste barriers:

- Absurd the castes; absurd their names;
- All living being, flourish under the same shadow;[24]
- Know the light,[25]
- Don't ask the caste, next there is no caste;[26]
- Next beauty and caste do not go;[27]
- One becomes, what one does;[28]
- Next there is no caste, nor strength;
- Next living beings are new;[29]
- Light[30] in every caste, God is known in light.

Guru Nanak himself was born in a higher caste in a noble [Hindu] family and Hinduism is *Varnashrama* i.e. it believes in *Varnas* [i.e. castes] and *Ashramas* [i.e. stages of life]. But in his preaching and practices he rejected the barriers of caste and the division of life. He had stressed the necessity of leading a householder's life. However, the five cardinal virtues i.e. purity, self-control, detachment, truth and non-violence which are to be cultivated by all Hindus, have been considered essential for his disciples by the Guru. He astounded everybody when he said:

- ♦ Nanak enjoys their company and does not vie with the superior ones;
- ♦ Where the lowly are taken care of, there is bestowed your generosity.[31]

Thus by virtue of his love for mankind irrespective of the differences created by the caste and community, he could build bridges between man and man and bring about reconciliation among different people. An example of the high regard in which he was held by the people is provided by his visit to Mecca the central place of - Mohammedanism. At that time all Arab lands were under Ottomans. The Turks had prohibited the navigation of the Red Sea by all Non-Muslim vessels lest these should even distantly pollute the holiest shrine of Mohammedanism in Mecca. However, Guru Nanak not only was admitted to the holiest shrine, but exchanged views with the Muslim head priest and was not molested. He preached his message of peace and reconciliation in the Muslim countries of West Asia.

For him, man was the same irrespective of whether he was a Hindu, Muslim or follower of some other religious community or born of a different caste or race. In the eyes of God all were equal; such was the case with Guru Nanak.

We have said in the preceding pages that Sikhism regarded the state as aggressor and oppressor owing to the nature of the system prevailing in the medieval age. What sort of rule did the Sikh Gurus preach as a model to avoid human suffering and blood-shed on account of disturbed peace?

- ♦ The vow of the conscious in knowledge, a recluse's vow the celibacy;
- ♦ *Brahmin's* vow in contentment, householder's vow the charity;

- Ruler's vow the justice and the learner's vow judicious inclination;[32]
- *Ram Raj* [God's rule] at Ramdaspur is established by the *Guru*;
- Nanak! The enemy's fear is banished by praising *'Na' 'am'*;[33]
- Benign [God] has commanded; no one displeases anyone;
- The subjects are in comfort, this is the rule of humility;[34]
- Mind, is controlled, it now has treasures of pearls, truth is never blemished;
- *Raja* retains the throne, if he is imbued with five fine qualities;[35]
- Himself he has created throne; sky and underworld" [upper and nether Worlds];
- By his command earth is created as a *Dharmshala*;[36]
- This is *Guru's*; Govind's eternal city comfort is attained by recitation of *'Na' 'am'*;
- Coveted fruits were gained; Creator himself has established it;

- God himself has colonised it, all comforts have been gained;
- Sons, Brothers and Sikhs are pleased;
- House, *mandirs* [temples] and shop centres are good looking;
- All beings live in comfort, God himself is the protector.[37]

These are only sample quotations from the *Gurubani* to illustrate that the *Gurus* not only preached, but they established model cities to show by a practical demonstration how a state should run. The *Gurus* had founded some townships but Amritsar [originally] named Ramdaspur after the name of the fourth Guru Ramdass, was the central point of Sikh activity.

That is why; Amritsar was called by Guru Arjun as the Rule of humility. This was in direct contrast to the prevailing view that the *Raja* by nature was aggressive and annexationist. In those days, the *Raja* and the state were synonymous. If the principles prescribed for a *Raja* [ruler] or the state were strictly and meticulously adhered to, there would not be aggression by any state upon another and no disturbance of peace among nations would take place. Moreover, the ruler, and the state power in the internal administration would not be violent against the subjects. Full justice would prevail; justice leavened with benevolence. Guru Amar Dass the third Sikh Guru has prescribed:

- Only that Raja should sit on the throne who is worthy of throne;
- Who have acknowledged truth are true *Rajas* [rulers];
- They are not landowners, *Rajas* who harm in the quest for other temptations.[38]

Having briefly given the basic principles prescribed by *Gurubani* [sayings and writings of the Sikh *Gurus* and contemporary Hindu saints] for the rulers and the state structure, it now remains for us to give the basic principle of *Gurubani* on which the world order should be organised. Actually, state and the *Raja* [ruler] were both very important because they functioned to implement the laid down ideals. But what should be the principle which they should apply in actual working of the state and the administration? Guru Nanak set the pace for laying down the dictum:

- In-Law's, Property is all common;
- In parental home, the woman is separatist;
- Herself she unmannerly and does not know how to take care of it.[39]

This is rather a difficult passage to fully understand. *Gurubani* like Bible is mostly parabolic. The human soul is often referred to as a woman who has to go from her parent's house on marriage to the house of her in-laws where she has to live for the rest of her life. The early premarital life has to be devoted by her assiduously for acquiring these virtues which would fit her to married life's paradox that in this world all human beings are separatists and individualistic, but in the eyes of God all material for human use in common to all and no exception is made. Guru Arjun Dev was, however, more explicit on this issue. He stated:

"*All are called co-sharers, no one is excluded.*"[40]

Thus all the material offered by God's nature is common to all mankind; none should, therefore, be excluded from his equal share of the gifts of God.

In actual life, the *Gurus* preached the concept of *Hindustan*. For them, *Hindustan* was not a congeries of state fighting against each other. They made sacrifices for the sake of humanity. Theirs was a world concept in which each country was flourishing along with all the countries. The underlying principle was:

"*Why are you attached to your family? All this in the orchard of rose flowers.*"[41]

That is, flowers are to be enjoyed for their beauty and fragrance and are not to be plucked. There should be no room for attachment and ownership in life. All material things are for human use and their distribution for use should be just. The *Gurus* realized that this was an uphill task, but the ideal should be laid down so that quest for justice should be prescribed as the remedy for all our ills. The Gurus realised that justice was something like will of the wisp, something unattainable by man. A quote:

"*See one miracle, my dear! Whatever God does is celestial justice.*"[42]

That is, man's world, justice is a miracle and miracle is possible only by God. World peace is impossible without justice in national and international affairs. But man is not capable of dealing out justice.

◊ CONCLUSION

Sikhism has its down distinctive theology, philosophy and mysticism. It is a 'faith of hope and cheer, through which the *Khalsa*, with secular ambitions while containing to be an integral constituent of the world, can yet remain distinctive and thus '*be entitled to conferment of all glory*'. The sword of a Sikh is neither for enslaving others nor for oppression; it is the sword for liberty and freedom, this is the concept of non-violence of the Sikhs. With this it is also linked the doctrine of *Hukam* [or *raja*] accepting which a person could even achieve martyrdom.

Free from prejudice of race and colour, and modest proud of its precepts, as codified in the *Guru Granth Saheb*, which permeate Sikh thought and mould a Sikh's temperament, Sikhism is a religious community of black and white alike, is not contemptuous of other doctrines. "T*olerance of other faiths is a principle of Sikhism and there are injunctions to the effect that only he is a perfect Sikh who accords "full respect to a stranger*" i.e. a person of other community or nationality.

Sikhism develops a character of courage, ready for sacrifice, idealistic with instinctive adherence to democracy, patriotism of the highest order.

A Sikh practices the following which attributes to universal peace and a balanced world order:

NAM SIMRAN	:	To mediate on his name-purification of thought;
KIRAT KARNA	:	To earn his bread through honest labour; and
VANDCHHAKNA	:	To share with the needy.

Sikhism is a character for peace in the world. I quote a *Shabad* of Saint Ravi Dass, appeared in *Guru Granth Saheb* in which he expresses his desire for a city of peace where everybody enjoys equal happiness:

- The name of the city is *Begumpura*, i.e. a city without sorrow;
- There is no place for pain or anxiety there;
- No care of any tribute or tab or property;
- There is no fear or sin, nor dread of a fall; and
- There is no second or third, all are equal.

In the end I mention another *Shabad* from *Guru Granth Saheb*[43] which directs the people to the path of world peace:

- Forgot the jealousy for other;
- Since I joined *Sadh Sangat* [Company of *Sadhus*];
- For me none an enemy, none a stranger, I've peace with everyone;
- I have got good advice from *sadhus* [saints] to accept as good whatever God does;
- God is immanent in everything; Nanak is joyful on seeing this.

References

1. *Prabhali Bibhas*, Kabir p. 1349
2. Nanak, *Var Asa*, p. 466.
3. The age when *Kali* worship was accepted by *Aryans* in their pantheism.
4. Guru Ram Dass, Asa, p. 445
5. Guru Nanak, *Majh*, p. 148
6. Holy book of the Hindus.
7. Nanak, *Ramkali*, p. 951
8. An official under Muslim rule who implemented royal order.
9. Guru Nanak, Ramkali, page, 902.
10. It is a fact that many birds and wild animals are trained for help in catching their own kind. In the same way, *Sikdars* also helped the rulers to catch their fellowmen.
11. A scholar versed in Hindi scriptures and learning of every description.
12. A junior revenue official in Mughal rule whose job was to help in tax collection and also maintain revenue records.
13. Guru Nanak, *Malhar*, page. 1288.
14. Guru Nanak, *Asa*, page, 418.
15. *Khurasan* was the name of the country expending from the Suleiman ranges deep into Central Asia. Kandhar, Herat, Meshod and Merve were the main centres. This country was named Afghanistan by Ahmed Shah Abdali in 1747 when he carved out a separate kingdom for himself after the assassination of Nadir Shah in June, 1747.
16. Guru Nanak, Asa, page, 360.
17. The central worship place of Mohammedanism.
18. Guru Nanak, *Var Majh*, page, .40.
19. These are not the real names of the five namazes, but these are names arising out the qualities which Guru Nanak ascribes to them.
20. The basic 'Mantra' of the Muslim faith.
21. Guru Nanak, Var Majh, page, 140.
22. The rust is of sins which soul is carrying through transmigration.
23. Guru Arjun, *Gauri*, page, 319-20.

24. Guru Nanak, *Sri Rag*, page. 83.

25. Heavenly light which shines in every human mind, but is blurred by human ignorance, thus mankind gropes its way in the dark.

26. Guru Nanak, *Asa*, page, 349.

27. Next world. That is, next life, Sikhism strongly believes in transmigration.

28. It is the cardinal tenet of Sikhism that actions of man give his mind a certain colour. Different colours, of different action help to produce a certain hue, which determines our next life after death. From Amar Dass, *Asa*, page, 363.

29. Of different nature and different built.

30. Guru Nanak, *Asa*, page, 469.

31. Guru Nanak, *Majh*, page,13.

32. Prevailing notion of that age; government was by rule arrogant. The established model colonies to give practical proof; rule of humility also could prevail. From Guru Nanak, *Sarang*, page, 1240.

33. Guru Arjun. *Bilawal*, page. 817.

34. Guru Arjun. *Sri Rag*, page. 74.

35. The five qualities are: *Satya* [truth] *Santokh* [contentment and sobriety], kindness, piety, restraint. Guru Nanak, *Maru*, page, 991.2.

36. A place where .people gather for collective good and religious practices, Guru Amar Dass, *Soohi,* page, 85.

37. Guru Arjun, *Soohi*, page, 783.

38. Guru Amar Dass, *Maru*, page, 1088.

39. Guru Nanak, *Basant,* page, 1171.

40. Guru Arjun, *Majh*, page, 91.

41. Guru Arjun, *Sri Rag*, page. 50.

42. Guru Arjun, *Bihagra*, page, 541.

43. Guru Arjun, *Kanra*, page, 1299.

CHAPTER-7
ZOROASTRIANISM

Incorporation of Active Goodness for All Round Development of All

"Only one Ahura Mazda[1] there is. He is Lord of life and knowledge... He is supreme and is epitome of ultimate peace. He is one and only one. Consciousness, Truth, Justice, Reality, Love and Compassion emerge only as per His being. Man should worship Him and may peace be unto man."

The propounder of Zoroastrianism- Spitama Zoroaster's above-mentioned dictum accords unity of humanity and thereby puts a human being as a bead in rosary: the rosary can be compared to world peace. As we are already in the knowledge of a single God theory of total faith in such a divine system, this philosophy enunciates whole humanity to be part of God. All being His part happen to be equal. No one should be termed big or small. All must worship Him and should try to be His achiever: this only is state of peace.

Spitama Zoroaster was born ab out 2000 B.C. in *Aryan* Clan in Southern Iran. Social and religious conditions were full of utter complexities at that time. Man was under darkness of sanctimoniousness then. He was extremely involved in sacrificing animals in the name of gods and in other forms. There existed an evil of Black Magic and every human being was sad owing to that. Many social evils were stated to be right under the name of religion. Intoxication had also been one of the evils. There was darkness at individual, social and national planes. Man was victim of non-peace. He was sad and was surrounded by difficulties.

Zoroaster experienced all this at an early age. He began to ponder over this grief when he was only fifteen years of age. He gave up worldly pleasures which actually happened to be the cause of grief and turmoil and began to pursue peace. He became twenty after five years and now after renunciating home, he began to think deeply of taking abode in a cave. He continued to think in this manner for ten years and ultimately he gained knowledge at the age of thirty.[2] subsequently, he began to tread path of peace and as a Prophet imparted message for the peace of world.

What is the message? How can we get real pleasure after getting rid of grief and can be able to establish peace in the world? Towards this, Zoroaster put the most significant fact on oneness of human beings before us. He prescribed that we all are offspring of single God. As such, human beings must learn to be united with love and co-operation. In other words, he took human unity to be supreme and stated single God purview to be the basis of this. This is really a very important and handsome step in the direction of establishment of world peace. In addition to that, other significant messages in Zoroastrian philosophy for this purpose are:

◊ A. TRUE ACTION

Zoroaster said about two types of actions: True and False. Every human being happens to be in the midst of true and false both. This can be compared to a bridge in the midst of two banks. A bridge separates two banks as well as it unites them. In the same way, man can separate true and false actions and can also bring them together. In case a man aspires for prosperity and state of peace, he must indeed tend towards true actions. This remains to be full of goodness and attributes of welfare. In his very words:

"*Pleasure, peace, disaster...all result from good [truthful] or bad [false] deeds of man.*"

He also gave a message that one can be near to God by true actions only. This also indicates existence of humanity. It clearly means that man's existence depends upon true actions. As such, a man will have to perform true actions if he aspires for peace. False action is at the root of grief.

◇ B. LIBERALITY AND FRATERNITY

Zoroaster emphasised liberality and fraternity along with human unity. His highly remarkable and real message was:

"*In case a man adopts fraternity in real sense and keeps a pace with liberal policy along with that, he gives himself unto that spirit of equality which is liked by his God and which imparts peace to him.*"

He not only gave his message but applied it in his practices and, as such presented very good examples before human world. In Zoroastrian treatises, there is mentioned a good episode in this context and it can be cited as an example here. There had been very severe famine on earth in the age of Zoroaster. All were under its attack. Grief of already grief-stricken became unbound. Many of them died. His parents were wealthy and so he urged them to distribute all amongst poor and depressed. His parents did so. Everything was distributed. Now the family of Zoroaster became equally poor. This was a unique example of liberality, fraternity and equality. He continued to impart this very message throughout his life; it was not an act limited to message giving alone-he treated this path practically in life.

◊ C. LIBERTY

A man in chains can never prosper in any field of life. Not only that, a dependent one cannot develop himself spiritually. It is on this count that Zoroastrian philosophy highly applauded human liberty. Topics related to human liberty have been there more than once in *Avesta*[3] and in all of them he has been accorded right to this. Man is free in this world to know darkness and light, good and bad; justice and injustice and truth and non-truth. He is at liberty to understand and adopt good and bad. God Himself granted this freedom to man. But as we get a handsomely good fruit in future if we sow a handsomely good plant at present, in the same way- the actions carried out with the spirit of fairness, justice and truth accord us prosperity and peace. It is the duty of man to know this and act accordingly. This is the way of enlightenment.

Human liberty has really been given foremost position in Zoroastrian philosophy. Liberty has been preferred not only in worldly practices but also in sphere of summum bonum that is ultimate good sphere. It has been described:

"*Almighty wants His offspring to be near Him...but with self-will and affectionately.*"

◊ D. MERCY AND FRIENDLINESS

"*Man should have the spirit of mercy not only towards man but unto every living being and this mercy must imbibe itself with the spirit of friendliness"*, Zoroaster called upon this 'humanity' in his message. Mercy and friendliness together constitute compassion. Compassion occupies an important place in eternal human values. It was on this count that Zoroaster declared as inhuman the customs of sacrifice and violence prevalent in his time and also declared them to be symbolic of non-peace. He declared:

"*Mercy and friendliness are indicative of humanity. Man cannot be perfect in the absence of them.*"

In this way, Zoroaster called upon man to imitate the way to peace while imparting him knowledge of eternal human values like liberty, mercy, friendliness, fraternity, truthfulness and equality. Who can deny that these eternal values shall not bring all-sided development of man and will not promise a position of peace unto him? It is, of course, imperative that behaviour should be conducted in accordance with these values 'Good, that is-sacred thoughts, good words and talks and good actions of sacred nature are necessary to achieve this ambition.' This is the purpose -cum- meaning of the main principles in Zoroastrian philosophy: *Humata, Hukta, Huvarashta or Manashmi, Gavashmi* and *Kunashmi.*

Zoroastrian philosophy incorporates active goodness as the most important point. This philosophy aims at making all-sided development of man who can be termed well as per above mentioned main values and Godly grace. A man, so all-sided developed, can only be an inspirator of peace. In this way, we can briefly state that this philosophy is also dedicated to good actions and human unity resultant to international peace.

References

1. God
2. Like Lord Buddha's and *Thirthankara* Mahavira's thoughts, main thing in Spitama's thought was to know about the mystery. This relates to questions as to why there is misery in the world. Why death.....? Why are some oppressed and hungry, Whereas some are rich and prosperous?. Why any evil, whatsoever, cropped in this world, et cetera?
3. 'Avesta'- is the main religious treatise of Zoroastrian philosophy.

■■■

CHAPTER-8
CONCLUSION

Concluding Observation Some Suggestions

In the light of our discussion of seven religious communities— Buddhism, Christianity, Hinduism, Islam, Jainism, Sikhism and Zoroastrianism - and the peace, our different analysis and our definition of religion perceived through Hinduism, we arrived at some common conclusion that a general and fundamental spirit prevails through all religious communities. If we find that there is difference between what one faith preaches from that of the other, we are to blame ourselves for it because we see only the outer dissimilarities between the two. We, in fact, are unable to understand the true meaning and spirit of religion and if we try to get to the real meaning of religion we shall find that all the religious faith start from a point and in the long run reach the same goal of common welfare, upliftment of the masses and strength of people. In fact, the fault lies not with faith or its preachers but we are to be blamed for the obstacles that we ourselves create in our path because of wrongful thinking and actions.

Religion is utilized for properly moulding and directing human life. Thus religion is what is adopted. Now, the question is what is to be adopted and how to be adopted? The answers to these questions are adoption of goodness and that too without any hesitation. Moreover, an individual, along with adoption of a faith in his life should let others do so because if we wish to make our life peaceful and harmonious, it is essential that we should let others live harmoniously and peacefully. It is also essential that we should co-operate in the achievement of this goal. We should not, in any circumstances, think or imagine of praying for peace for ourselves alone. If we do so, it shows our ignorance.

If to adopt goodness is religion, can the scope of goodness be limited? Can goodness for somebody prove to be evil for someone else? In my opinion, it is never so because goodness always remains goodness; it is as it is for everybody. Goodness is for the commonweal because it is excellent in nature. That is why I strongly believe that the religion is excellent. Nobody is inferior or bad. There is nothing bad if due to variation of time and circumstances there is a variation in the way of reaching a common goal. After all, the common goal is peace for everyone. I am reminded of an instance given by H. H., the Dalai Lama and find his words quite appropriate for praying for peace. He says, "*All faiths agree upon the necessity to control the undisciplined mind that harbours selfishness and other roots of trouble, and each teaches a path leading to a spiritual state that is peaceful, disciplined, ethical and wise*."

The aim of religion is to shape life in a proper mould and for this purpose all the chief religious communities believing in the supremacy of God have emphasized over the unity of mankind. We have found this very clearly during our analysis of Islam, Hinduism, Christianity, Sikhism and Zoroastrianism. The communities like Jainism and Buddhism which do not believe in the supremacy of God, in spite of their being atheists, emphasise on shaping human life in a proper mould. They, analyse the miseries of human beings, reason thereof and way and means to eliminate them, and very clearly hint at a path leading to a harmonious life. What a great coincidence that both- atheist and theist- religious communities agree on the points as to how to establish peace in the world, where is the contradiction?

We have to think over our ignorance. How do the goals differ? We have to consider our duties and right from a religious angle and have to re-establish them.

II

Mankind shows the existence of human society and in order to maintain the existence of humanity, our march towards universal peace is unavoidable. Man's soul itself pines for peace and marching contrary to it, disobeying its dictate. Therefore, every faith talks of strengthening the soul.

Greek philosopher Plato, in his Republic, has remarked to the extent that keeping in life injustice and other evils strongly is weakening and killing the soul and if this act of strengthening of evil is continued, the soul keeps in readiness to take fight from the body. Injustice and evil are at the root of conflict whereas soul hints at peace.

Considering from the intellectual view point, we find that a disturbed human life is at the root of all blemishes, difficulties and troubles and religion all the time tries to salvage the human life from these troubles, difficulties and blemishes. Thus considering from the point of view of humanity we find that ultimate goal of religion is the establishment of harmony and ultimate peace. The fundamentals of humanity- brotherhood, cooperation and unity-are found alike in every religious faith. Therefore, throughout our previous analysis, we have not found anywhere religious faith creating gulf between human beings. On the other hand, the following conclusion emerge everywhere:

- All religious faiths bring the message of love, mutual understanding and peaceful coexistence based not only on political ideology but emerging out of the true religious tenets;
- Every faith opposes a life based on falsehood. It can

never compromise with blemishes, evils and misconducts;

- A true faith can never be silent on untruth, impurity and evil while establishing a truthful human life as it is especially clear in the chapter dealing with Sikhism;
- It is the object of religious communities to make its followers aware of the purpose of life. Thus teachings of a religious community provide a base to a life. It regulates the life of an uncontrolled and directionless man, and while doing so it does not create obstacles in the way of his progress and capabilities;
- Every religious community shuns violence. Propounder of every religious community has given the message of non-violence. None has advocated violence;
- A theist community believes that we all are the children of God and it is our duty to take care of each other and share one another's joy and sorrows. God is one although his names are countless. The atheist community believes that there is no difference betwixt human beings. To share others' grief is the duty of man so this is the ultimate truth. The theist and the atheist both concur on this point;
- Every community directs man to the path of peace so that human life, instead of getting trapped into evils, should tread the path leading to peaceful life of comforts and prosperity. On this very path lies his duties to his family, to the society, to the nation and to the whole of the world;
- There is no denying the fact that different religious faiths, despite their inherent differences of opinions, ask their followers to share the grief of other human beings

and also to work for the progress of mankind and universal peace; and

- Another common point among the religious communities accepting the supremacy of God is that they emphasise faith in Almighty God and faith in love of God, as their purpose is the fulfilment of God's intentions. Seeing us all as creation and followers of one God, they teach that we should care about and help each other. The very purpose of faithful belief in God is to accomplish his wishes, the essence of which is to care about, respect, love and give service to our fellow humans.

III

Every religious community emphatically calls upon the human beings for universal peace. Forbearance, tolerance and concept of *Vasudhaiv Kutumbakam*- the world is one family, of Hinduism; Islam's emphasizing upon the brotherhood, Christianity's advocacy of love and service; compassion and non-violence of Buddhism and Jainism respectively; Sikhism's vow to remove injustice bravely and considering all human beings as one and concept of unity from Zoroastrianism, are, more or less similar methods of establishing peace in the world.

The invisible link betwixt religion and peace, and its beings repeated again and again is not new as it has been emphasized by Prophets, *Avtaras* and *Rishis* time and again. There are certain facts which help us to move our steps towards this eternal truth established by religious communities. I would like to conclude this discussion with the following observations:

- If a man is at peace, he can see peace everywhere. In order to establish peace steps of multitude shall precede those of an individual and moving along with this path is what religion preaches;

- All the religious preachers must carefully consider what their religious faith preaches. Fanaticism shall have to be shaded. United efforts shall have to be made for the welfare of everybody so that a peaceful life can be achieved;
- Force can never establish peace because peace accomplished through the use of force shall involve sacrifice of one party. That party shall be rendered bitter and thus there can be no peace. The efforts to bring peace through understanding and desire are much more real and better than those bringing peace through methods adopting force because the former are based on mutual acceptance;
- Leaving aside the feelings of caste, creed, gender, community and nation the followers of different religious communities should practice the feeling of love which is at very basis of all the religious faiths. Love is that power which is synonymous to unity along with peace;
- If love is at the basis of all religious faiths, love and peace are the two sides of a coin. Since kindness is a part of peace, we should not turn away from the fundamental qualities of love and kindness;
- We must inculcate compassionate thoughts in order to see the mankind live through peace and love; and
- Good motivation is a very important basis of religion. Thus we have to depend on it for the sake of mankind. Without good motivation, the modern scientific and technical achievements shall, instead of giving us progress and prosperity, push us towards annihilation.

APPENDIX

The Prohibitions for The Establishment Of Permanent Peace in The World as Laid Down in *Shrimad Bhagvad-gita*

◊ **The Prohibited Acts:**

In any way whatsoever, through mind, speech and body, the acts prohibited by the scriptures such as theft, adultery, deception, fraud, falsehood, oppression, violence, wrongdoing, taking of interdicted food etc. must be renunciated:

◊ **Worldly Desires Prohibited:**

Sacrifices, charities, austerities, worship and other desire born actions with a selfish motive for gaining objects of enjoyment, such as wife, progeny and wealth etc., or with the object of terming various forms of suffering, must totally be renunciated.

◊ **Worldiy Achievement Prohibited:**

Dignity, fame, social prestige, wife, progeny, wealth and all objects automatically gained by the force of '*Prarabdha*' or destiny must be renunciated, holding them as an obstacle in the way of the realization of God.

◊ **Habit of Extracting Service from Others with a Selfish Motive Prohibited:**

Demanding service from another for personal happiness, asking money, and acceptance of things and service given unasked or entertaining any desire for getting by any means one's self interest served by another, all these and similar ideas of getting service from another for the satisfaction of self interest must be prohibited.

◇ Prohibition of Indolence and Desire for Fruit:

In the performance of all duties, such as cultivation of devotion of God, worship, service to parents and all other elders, performance of sacrifice [for the cause of humanity], charities and austerities, maintenance of the household assigned according to the *Varnashrama Dharma* and taking of food and drink etc. for maintaining sound health, indolence in any form and desire for attaining worldly pleasures should be prohibited.

◇ The Sense of *Meum* and Attachment Prohibited:

The feeling of Meum and attachment in connection with all worldly objects like wealth, house, clothes, etc.; all relations like wife, children, friends etc.; and all sort of enjoyment of this world and the next life; fame, prestige, honour, dignity etc. must totally be abandoned. Having abandoned the sense of *Meum* and attachment, man's distaste for wasting even a moment of his valuable time in the company of men attached to the world and indulging in laughter, luxury, carelessness, enjoyment, backbiting and idle talk become automatically developed.

◇ Subtle Desire and Egotism Prohibited:

All worldly objects being creation of *Maya* are totally perishable and only one indestructible God equally pervades everywhere. Holding this notion as true, all suitable desires with regard to worldly objects, including the body and the actions thereof must totally be prohibited. In other words, due to total lack of identification with the body, there should be no sense of worship with regard to all actions done through mind, speech and body.

GLOSSARY

Avatar	:	Incarnation; decent
Dhammapada	:	A collection of teachings of Lord Buddha
Dharma	:	Duty; what is to be held or kept or adopt; the complex of religious and social obligations which a devout Hindu is required to fulfil.
Jeevan	:	Life; existence; lifetime; livelihood
Karma	:	Action; deed; work; occupation; function
Karmic	:	One who act or work
Mahayana	:	A sect of Buddhism lying emphasis on the propagation aspect
Maya	:	Essence; substance; wealth; means; firmament; leaven
Meum	:	I; to be egotistical; full of oneself
Pada	:	Pace; step; trace; position; post; a verse
Prarabdha	:	Fate; destiny; caused by fate;
Sukha	:	Happiness; pleasure; joy; comfort; convenience; prosperity; relief
Varnashrama Dharma	:	The particular socio-religious duty of members of each of the four *Varnas* in the four stages of life of Hindus

BIBLIOGRAPHY

- Azad, Abul Kalam, Qur'an Ka Sandesh, M. A. M. A., Lucknow, First Hindi Edition, 1990.
- Abbott, Justin E., Godbole, N. R. and Edwards, J. F., Nectar [Translated by], from Indian Saints, Poona, 1935.
- Archer, John Clark, The Sikh in Relation to Hindus, Moslems, Christians and Ahmadiyas: A Study in Comparative Religion, Princeton University Press, Princeton, 1946.
- Banerjee, Indubhushan, Evolution of the *Khalsa* [Volume-I], Calcutta, 1936.
- Behari Bankey, *Sufis*, Mystics and *Yogis* of India, Bhartiya Vidya Bhavan, Bombay, 1962.
- Benveniste, E., The Persian Religion According to the chief Greek Texts, paris, 1929.
- Bettany, G. T., Encyclopaedia of World Religions, Victoria Books International, Delhi, Reprint 1991.
- Bloomfield, M., [Translated by], Hymns of the *Atharva-Veda*, Atlantic, New Delhi, 1990.
- Boyce, M., History of Zoroastrianism, 1975.
- Buhler, George, The Sacred Laws of the *Aryans*, Volume I & II, APD, New Delhi, 1990
- Bulky, V. [Translated by], *Pavitra Bible* [in Hindi], Hindi Sahitya Sammitee, Allahabad, 1985.
- Carus, Paul, The Gospel of Buddha, Publications Division, Government of India, New Delhi, Reprint, 1990.
- Caveeshar, Sardul Singh, Guru Nanak and World Peace, National Publications, Lahore, 1937.

- Caveeshar, Sardul Singh, The Sikh Studies, National Publications, Lahore, 1937.
- Chaturvedi, Jwala Prasad, [Translated by], *Manusmriti,* Randhir Books, Haridwar, Third Edition, 1992.
- Chennakesaven, Saraswati, A Critical Study of Hinduism, Motilal Banarsidas, Delhi, 1974.
- Cowbell, E. B., and others [Translated by], Buddhist *Mahayana* Text, Atlantic, New Delhi, 1990.
- Earle, William James, Introduction to Philosophy, McGraw-Hill, Inc. New York, 1992.
- Eggeling. J., The *Shatapatha Brahmana*, Volume I to V, APD, New Delhi, 1990.
- Gallie, W. B., Philosophers of Peace and War, Cambridge University Press, 1978.
- Gandhi, M. K., Essence of Hinduism, Navajivan, Publishing House, Ahmedabad, 1987.
- Gandhi, M. K., India of My Dreams, Navajivan Publishing House, Ahmedabad, 1980.
- Howard, I. K. A., [Translated by], *Kitab Al-Irshad* [of S. al-Mufid], Ansariyan Publication, Qum, Iran, 1981.
- Imam Ali, *Nahjul Balagha*, [Sermons, Lectures and Sayings], Ansariyan Publications, Qum, Iran, 1981.
- Jacobi, Hermann, [Translated by], *Jaina Sutras*, Part I & II, APD, New Delhi, 1990.
- Jittasubho, Luangpor Teean, Teacher-Teaching, L. T. J. Foundation, Bangkok, Thailand, 1997.
- Jolly Julius [Translated by], The Institutes of Visnu, Atlantic, New Delhi, 1990.

- Joshi, V. M., Kathopnishadh, S. S. V. K., Ahmedabad, 1980.
- Kalelkar, Kakasaheb, *Yuganukul Hindu Jeevandrishti*.
- Max Muller F., [Translated by], The *Dhammapada*, Atlantic Publishers and Distributors, New Delhi, 1990.
- Max Muller F., [Translated by], The *Upanishads*, Part I & II, APD, New Delhi, 1990.
- Max Muller F., [Translated by], *Vedic* Hymns, Part I & II, APD, New Delhi, 1990.
- M. Farooq Khan, *Hadis Saurabh* [in Hindi], M. M. I., Delhi, Third Edition, 1985.
- Mishra, Shivgopal, [Translated by], *Bhagvad-Gita* As It Is, Bhaktivedanta Book Trust, Mumbai, Third Hindi and English Editions, 1993.
- Neuner J., S. J. and Dupuis, J., S. J., [Edited by], The Christian Faith [In the Doctrinal Documents of the Catholic Church], Theological Publications in India, Fifth Edition, Bangalore, 1990.
- Palmer E. H., The Qur'an Part I & II, Atlantic, New Delhi, 1990.
- Pande, B. N., Hinduism and Islam, S. S. Academy, A. M. U., First Edition, 1988.
- Rhys, Davids T. W., [Translated by], *Buddhist Sutras,* Atlantic, New Delhi, 1990.
- Rhys, Davids T. W., The Questions of King Milinda, Volume I & II, APD, New Delhi, 1990.
- Schubring, Walter, The Doctrine of the *Jainas*, Motilal Banarsidas, Delhi, First Edition, 1962.

- S. Abul A'la Mawdudi, Towards Understanding the Qur'an [English Version of Tafhim Al-Qur'an], Volume I to III, M. M. I., Delhi, Reprint, 1994.
- Sagar, Mata Prasad, [Translated by], *Dhammapada*, Cultural Publishers, Lucknow, First Hindi Edition, 1985.
- Sankrityayan, Rahul, [Translated by], *Majjhimanikaya* [1], Mahabodhi Sabha, Banaras, 1933.
- Sen, Chatur, *Buddha Aur Boddh Dharm*a, Sanmarg, Delhi, 1986.
- Sharma, S., Rigveda, S. M. Aundh, First Edition, 1994.
- Shukla, B.N. Prasad, *Nanakvani* [Japuji], Lucknow, 1999.
- Singh, Harbans, *Guru Nanak Aur Sikh Dharam Ka Udvhav*, Punjabi University, Patiala, First Hindi Edition, 1971.
- Singh, Kapur, Sikhism for Modern Man, Guru Nanak Dev University, Amritsar, 1992.
- Singh, Ranbir, Glimpses of the Divine Masters, International Traders Corporation, New Delhi, 1965.
- Talib, Gurbachan Singh, [Translated by], *Sri Guru Granth Sahib*, Volume I to IV, Publication Bureau, Punjabi University, Patiala, First English Edition, 1990-95.
- Telang, K. T., *The Bhagavad-Gita*, Atlantic Publishers and Distributors, New Delhi, 1990.
- The Holy Qur'an [English Translation of the Meanings and Commentary], Kingdom of Saudi Arabia.

- Thibaut, G., The *Vedanta Sutras* [With Ramanuja's Sribhasya], Volume I to III, APD, Reprint, 1990.
- Tiwari, K. N., World Religions and Gandhi, Classical Publishing Company, New Delhi, First Edition, 1988.
- Verma, Prativa, Social Philosophy of the *Mahabharata* and the *Manusmirti,* Classical Publishing Company, New Delhi, 1988.
- Yandell, Keith, God, Man and Religion: Readings in the Philosophy of Religion, McGraw-Hill Book Company, New York, 1973.

INDEX